Divorce the IRS

Divorce

THE IRS

HOW TO DEFUSE YOUR
BIGGEST TAX TIME BOMBS
Before You Retire

JAMES MILLER
CRPC®

LIONCREST
PUBLISHING

DIVORCE THE IRS
How to Defuse Your Biggest Tax Time Bombs Before You Retire

ISBN   978-1-5445-2058-2   *Hardcover*
        978-1-5445-2038-4   *Paperback*
        978-1-5445-2037-7   *Ebook*

*For my mom, who has never stopped
encouraging me to save for the future.*

*For my dad, who taught me how important it
is to make a plan and stick with it.*

CONTENTS

PART III: WHAT TO DO ABOUT IT ALL

FOREWORD

I was first introduced to Jimmy by a mutual client of ours who wanted us to connect and discuss the tax implications of his current retirement strategy. As a tax practitioner specializing in consulting and compliance for US expats, this area can be particularly complex due to multiple taxing jurisdictions and the potential interplay of tax treaties. I jumped on the call expecting the same unsatisfactory outcome as when dealing with most financial service professionals. They normally understand as much of the extensive US tax code as any other US citizen, so that is to say they don't understand a lot!

From our very first phone call together, I knew Jimmy was different than most other professionals in his field. The most difficult part of my job on any given day is turning overly dense tax legalese into digestible explanations for my clients who are looking for guidance—and Jimmy was already several steps ahead. I was relieved to find a financial advisor who could not only grasp the tax consequences of various transactions and investments but actively advise on the ones likely to provide the best outcomes, no matter the goal of the client.

Speaking from the perspective of a practitioner in the tax field, Jimmy Miller is the ideal fiduciary financial advisor to work with and refer clients to. What I appreciate about Jimmy and this book is the holistic, long-term approach that is omnipresent and fundamental to his work. As evidenced by the contents of this book, he has a technical understanding of global tax implications as they relate to investing and retirement planning, which assists him in implementing a curated strategy for each of his clients.

Although a specific, long-term investment strategy is unique and circumstantial for everyone, this book serves as a tremendous resource for those looking to maximize their future retirement draws. You cannot find the valuable retirement tax planning advice packed into this book written as efficiently in any other. Although the themes are complex, Jimmy does a great job of explaining it in straightforward and actionable terms that adults in all phases of life will find useful. In reading this book, you will learn the strategies you should implement today to avoid paying more than necessary taxes to the IRS during your lifetime. Who wouldn't want that?

—NICHOLAS ROSCHER, CEO AND
FOUNDER OF REVOLVE TAX

Revolve Tax is a boutique accounting firm specializing in expat and international taxation for US taxpayers and businesses.

revolvetax.com

Part 1

UNDERSTANDING

INTRODUCTION

You have probably heard the phrase, "Nothing is certain but death and taxes." And while this is true, you may be able to do something about it—at least the tax part, anyway.

The United States tax code is over 74,000 pages long and contains over 3 million more words than the Bible. It's no wonder taxes are such a big issue in financial planning and why they are so misunderstood. They don't have to be, though, and it's even possible to divorce the Internal Revenue Service (IRS) completely and enjoy a tax-free retirement, if you plan properly.

No matter how patriotic, I have never met anyone who was happy about paying a tax bill, especially one they didn't expect. I suppose it's happened, though, like when someone wins the lottery or finds themselves in a similar circumstance. I do meet people all the time who are happy to get money back from the IRS, though. They don't usually understand that it's either their own money being returned (without interest) or it's a loan they will have to repay one day (most of the time, with interest).

I have been helping people with tax-free retirement planning for over twenty years now as an independent fiduciary financial advisor. I find that most Americans fail to create (or keep) real wealth. It's not that they plan to fail but that they fail to plan. There are a myriad of reasons for this, but the one I help with in this book is among the largest: the IRS.

Americans have to work, on average, the first 111 days of each year just to take care of their tax burden. You can find out more about this on this book's Resources page at Divorce-The-IRS.com. However, it's enough to know this led to The Tax Foundation creating Tax Freedom Day in America—the day when the nation as a whole has earned enough money to pay its total tax bill for the year. In 2021, Tax Freedom Day will fall on April 17. This fact, along with tax traps—or tax time bombs waiting for the unprepared— has led to the IRS taking a larger share of people's money than needed.

The Number of Days in 2021 that Americans as a Whole Worked to Pay Off Each Tax Type
America's Tax Bill Type/Source in Days

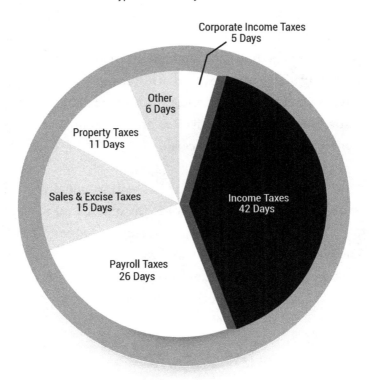

Have you ever noticed the words *the* and *IRS* combine to spell *theirs*? It doesn't have to be that way, though. Not completely, anyway.

This book is for those interested in a journey to a specific destination: divorcing the IRS on retirement day and enjoying a tax-free retirement.

This is a path to success, as defined by you, that can only be achieved with proper, modern financial planning and forward thinking. It requires you to save as much as possible through the lens of your entire life ahead, not just this year or the next. It needs a deliberate direction to minimize your obligation to the IRS, both in life and after. It will be an odyssey, preparing you financially for all the things life may throw at you so your wealth creation has minimal interruptions and no fatal experiences.

This journey will take you to a destination where you get to enjoy the fruits of your labor to the maximum, without the IRS interfering. You'll enjoy the feeling that comes with knowing you did things right and you're ahead of the game. It's a place where your delayed gratification and smart financial moves pay off exponentially.

There is a peace of mind that comes with knowing there won't be any hidden financial surprises in retirement with respect to tax bills and knowing that even if tax rates increase, you won't be affected.

If you want to understand (and avoid) the most common tax problems (or tax time bombs, as I think of them) that seriously impede the wealth creation and retention process in America, this book is for you. The IRS has become very good at figuring out ways to tax you and take your money. Some of their rules (tricks) deliberately entice you to set yourself up to pay them even more when you least expect it.

Written as a quick read in an easy-to-understand format, this book is not designed to be a comprehensive financial blueprint. It will point out the basics of what you should know about the most common tax time bombs and can save you a lot of money when applied correctly to your own financial life. Working with a competent fiduciary financial planner who specializes in tax-free planning will compound the positive effects of this book.

The earlier you are in your journey to financial independence, the more this book can help. The solutions and strategies presented can be implemented at any point in life, but due to government restrictions and contribution limits, the more time you have to implement these strategies, the better off you will be.

Tax time bombs can be a nasty experience, leaving a permanent mark on your bank account and on you as a person. You may have already experienced one or more or know someone who has. Maybe you think it will never happen to you or you know how to avoid them. However, it's the ones you never see coming until it is too late that hurt the worst.

The tax bombs in this book are presented in the order they are likely to detonate in your life. If you have already escaped or experienced some of them, just skip to the chapters that are still relevant to you. My hope is that you can use the information presented to begin tax-free financial planning and avoid paying more to the IRS than necessary.

In Part 1, we start with a common tax misconception and the concept of three tax buckets. Once this is clear, we move into understanding why tax deductions and tax-deferred accounts may not be in your best interest—at least, not as your only retirement savings strategy.

In Part 2, we discuss the eight biggest tax time bombs people set up for themselves (usually unintentionally) and how to avoid them, followed by strategies you can implement to defuse these tax bombs.

In Part 3, I explain how to find your ideal number—the exact amount of money you should have in tax-deferred accounts upon reaching retirement. This number will help you take advantage of the tax system and get as close to the 0 percent tax bracket in retirement as possible. Finally, I explain why tax preparers and most financial advisors, though well intentioned, are probably harming you with their advice.

By the end of this book, you will have the knowledge you need to avoid these wealth-destroying pitfalls, and you'll be able to turn the tables on the IRS. You'll have a plan to minimize your *total* lifetime tax payments, allowing you to keep most of what you did without for all of those years. When people start early enough with their planning, a 0 percent tax bracket throughout all of retirement is possible if the principles in this book are applied correctly. I hope that can be you.

As everyone's situation is different, this book is designed to be educational. It shouldn't be considered tax or legal advice. Consult a qualified fiduciary financial advisor (ideally one who specializes in tax-free retirement planning) and your tax consultant to discuss your unique situation. You may also contact us at Baobab Wealth Management, an independent, fee-based financial advisory practice I founded in 2015. We would be happy to help you with these issues within the context of a comprehensive financial plan.

Here are some fun facts you may not know about taxes:

1. In 2019, the US federal, state, and local governments collected a combined total of more than $5.3 trillion in taxes.
2. Taxpayers lose out on millions every year by not filing returns! In 2017, Americans gave up over $950 million in refunds owed to them by not filing.
3. Americans enjoy some of the lowest tax rates in the developed world. According to the Organization for Economic Cooperation and Development (OECD), the US ranks 26 out of 28 developed countries for tax burden.

4. Americans have to pay taxes in America even if they don't live there. The US is one of two countries in the world that taxes citizens worldwide.

By the end of this book, you'll feel pretty good about your understanding of foundational tax concepts. You will understand the tax time bombs waiting to explode in your life and how to defuse them. Most importantly, you will see it *is* possible to divorce the IRS and retire tax-free—as long as you plan for it. Let's start by examining the biggest tax misconception there is. I hear about it from almost everyone I speak with, and it has a huge impact.

Chapter 1

A TAX MISCONCEPTION

As a financial advisor, I get the opportunity to discuss topics like taxes with people almost every day. After more than twenty years in my profession, I have become acutely aware of how misunderstood taxes are, especially the way our progressive tax system works in America. And I know too many advisors (financial salespeople) who unfortunately take advantage of this fact. If you want to get yourself on a path to divorcing the IRS and achieving a tax-free retirement, you need to understand a few tax basics, including the biggest misconception around and the two measurements that are critical to tax planning.

Have you ever heard someone say they don't want a raise at work, or they don't want to work overtime because it would push them into a higher tax bracket? Have you heard them say it wouldn't be worth it, or they would actually lose money due to the taxes? This is a common misconception about tax brackets in America, and one people need to be educated about.

To put it very simply, if you make $1 over your tax bracket and it places you in the next tax bracket, you only pay the higher tax on that $1.

That is the simplest way to explain this concept. The misconception is that by piercing the higher tax bracket with that $1, *all* your money will now be taxed at that higher rate. That is simply false, and the idea needs to be eradicated. We have a progressive tax system in America, where the first part of your income is tax-free, and then, as income rises through brackets, the tax rate for each bracket rises.

This creates two different ways to measure your taxes, and these need to be understood before the remaining concepts in this book. If you already understand marginal and effective tax rates, then skip to the next chapter.

THE TWO TAX MEASUREMENTS

The two tax measurements are the marginal tax rate and the effective tax rate.

MARGINAL TAX BRACKETS

These are progressive tax brackets and are how most people think of and quote their tax rate. Once you have applied your itemized or standard deduction (the money you get to have tax-free), you then start into the marginal brackets. You only pay the tax rate for the dollars that fall into each bracket. Here are the 2021 bracket rates:

2021 Tax Brackets

Rate	Married Joint Return	Single Individual	Head of Household	Married Separate Return
10%	Up to $19,900	Up to $9,950	Up to $14,200	Up to $9,950
12%	Over $19,900	Over $9,950	Over $14,200	Over $9,950
22%	Over $81,050	Over $40,525	Over $54,200	Over $40,525
24%	Over $172,750	Over $86,375	Over $86,350	Over $86,375
32%	Over $329,850	Over $164,925	Over $164,900	Over $164,925
35%	Over $418,850	Over $209,425	Over $209,400	Over $209,425
37%	Over $628,300	Over $523,600	Over $523,600	Over $314,150

For an example of this in action, let's assume you have $50,000 of taxable income after applying your standard deduction, and you are filing single. You would then pay 10 percent on the first $9,950 and 12 percent on the income between $9,951 and $40,525. Then, you would pay 22 percent on the rest. The total bill would be about $6,750, which brings us to your effective tax rate.

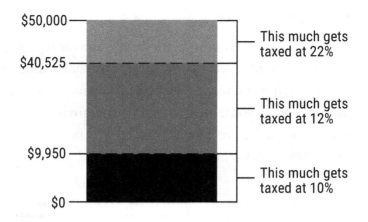

$50,000

$40,525 — This much gets taxed at 22%

This much gets taxed at 12%

$9,950

$0 — This much gets taxed at 10%

EFFECTIVE TAX RATE

Your effective tax rate is the average rate you paid on every taxable dollar you earned. This is the more important tax rate to understand, as it is a more accurate reflection of what you pay in taxes, and it evens the playing field when making comparisons or considering a tax strategy. Someone might make $1 in the 35 percent tax bracket (and pay 35 percent tax on that $1), but that hardly makes it accurate for them to say they pay 35 percent to the IRS (which is how most people talk about their taxes and tax brackets).

From our previous example, the $6,750 divided by the $50,000 of taxable income equals a 13.5 percent effective tax rate. So even though you ended up in the 22 percent tax bracket, you *effectively* paid 13.5 percent of your taxable income in taxes.

You have now had a short lesson in tax basics, breaking the misconception about tax brackets. Remember, we have a progressive tax system in the United States, and there are two tax measurements: marginal tax rate and effective tax rate. You know your effective tax rate is most useful in helping you understand your tax situation. Now that you are familiar with these basics which are critical to tax planning, let's move on to the concept of the three tax buckets.

Chapter 2

THE THREE TAX BUCKETS

When you earn income, you have a choice about where to put that money, assuming you haven't spent it all! There are many different types of accounts and investments, and they are not all created equal. They have different benefits and pitfalls. Thankfully, we do not need to discuss each and every type of bank account, investment product, and insurance policy, as they all fall into three main categories. In this chapter, we will review these categories—or buckets, as I call them—so you can start to see the opportunities they offer.

The three tax buckets that all accounts and investments fall into are "tax me now" (taxable), "tax me later" (tax-deferred), and "tax me never" (tax-free). What's important about these buckets are the types of accounts each one holds, not the actual investments. You can buy a stock or any investment in any of these three buckets. Which account you buy the investment in determines which bucket it goes into. Let's take a look at each one.

Nonqualified Bank, Brokerage Accounts	Tax-Deferred IRA, 401(k), 403(b), 457	Tax-Free Roth IRA, Roth 401(k), Roth 403(b), Life Insurance

THE "TAX ME NOW" BUCKET

The "tax me now" bucket, also called the non-qualified bucket, includes any type of account for which you receive a 1099 form on an annual basis. The money you deposit into these accounts (and the investments within these accounts) has already been taxed. You will only owe taxes annually on any growth, gains, or interest you realize in these types of accounts.

The most common type of "tax me now" accounts that almost everyone owns are bank accounts. The money you deposit into the bank has already been taxed. You get a 1099 from your bank each year declaring how much interest you made, which you need to include on your tax return so you can pay the taxes due.

Let's look at an example. If you have $50,000 in a one-year Certificate of Deposit (CD) at the bank, and it grows by 2 percent, you have a taxable event. At the end of the year, you will have $51,000, and you will have to pay federal and state tax (in most states) on every bit of that growth. So, $1,000 gets added right on top of all your other income for the year, and it's taxed at your highest marginal rate. Assuming you are in the 30 percent bracket (composed of 24 percent federal and 6 percent state tax, as an example), you would owe $300 in taxes. This means you didn't really experience $1,000 of growth, you only experienced $700. Thus, your after-tax rate of return on that $50,000 was only 1.4 percent. This annual taxation is one of the problems with the taxable bucket, as all of the interest isn't left to compound if you have to pay some of it to the IRS every year.

The other common accounts often found in the non-qualified "tax me now" bucket are regular (non-qualified) mutual funds or brokerage accounts. Those who want easy access to their money but prefer to invest in something with a higher potential return than a bank usually look to mutual fund or brokerage accounts. In a brokerage account, it is possible to invest in a plethora of investments like stocks, bonds, exchange-traded funds (ETFs), mutual funds, commodities, precious metals, real estate, and others. Although some of these investments don't get taxed annually but rather when they are sold, all are still taxable as gains are realized on them. Some investments in this bucket can also have more favorable tax treatment, like capital gains tax, which can be lower than ordinary income tax. It's great to learn more about capital gains tax, but it is beyond the scope of this book.

Why use accounts in the "tax me now" bucket? The answer is liquidity. The money that you generally have in taxable accounts, and thus "tax me now" type investments, is liquid. There is no penalty from the government for accessing this money. As many financial advisors will tell you, it's important to have at least three to six months' worth of living expenses stashed in an emergency fund. "Tax me now" bucket accounts are most suitable for this money. This bucket is also the most suitable for short-term savings goals, like a down payment on a home, a new car, or a wedding.

THE "TAX ME LATER" BUCKET

The "tax me later" bucket, also called the tax-deferred bucket, is the most popular bucket for retirement savings and the one that will absolutely tie you to the IRS forever. If you want to divorce the IRS one day, this is *not* where you want to save most of your money!

This bucket includes any retirement accounts to which you have contributed money on a pre-tax basis, such as most

IRAs, 401(k)s, and 403(b)s. There are others, as well, that have different rules, like the SEP, SIMPLE, Keough, and 457 plans.

This is probably the bucket you contribute the most money to. And why not? Out of sight, out of mind. This bucket makes saving for the future easy, plus, everyone is doing it, so it seems like a no-brainer. Plus, you save a little on your taxes along the way. Nice. Well, maybe not as nice as you think, as we will soon explore.

No matter the type of "tax me later" account you use, you'll find they generally have three things in common:

1. **Contributions are pre-tax.** Generally, when you contribute money to any of the accounts in this bucket, it is done pre-tax, and you receive a tax deduction for the contribution. For example, if you make $120,000 this year, and you put $10,000 into your traditional 401(k), your taxable income becomes $110,000.

2. **Growth is tax-deferred.** As you earn interest and experience growth from the underlying investments in the accounts, you don't have to pay any taxes. All the tax will be collected later when you withdraw money from these accounts.

3. **Withdrawals are considered ordinary or provisional income.** You pay taxes on the money—*all* the money— you take out of these accounts as if you earned it at a job

(minus Social Security and Medicare tax). You also pay taxes on the money at whatever your state and federal tax rates happen to be the year you take the withdrawal.

Many have likened the "tax me later" bucket to the concept of a farmer having a choice as to when he has to pay taxes. Do you think a farmer would like to pay tax on his handful of seeds or on his crop? Most would say paying on the seeds would be wiser, giving him a tax-free crop to harvest later on. But by putting money into the tax-deferred bucket, he is forgoing tax on the seeds for the liability of paying taxes on the entire crop one day!

THE "TAX ME NEVER" BUCKET

Finally, the "tax me never" bucket, also called the tax-free bucket, is a key point of this book. This bucket includes accounts to which you contribute after-tax money for retirement, such as Roth IRAs, Roth 401(k)s, Life Insurance Retirement Plans (LIRPs), and others. You do not get any special tax breaks upfront with this bucket, but all contributions and growth can be withdrawn income-tax-free for qualified reasons. (This generally means you are at least 59.5 years old and have had the account for at least five years). Using this bucket is like the farmer choosing to pay tax on the seeds and no tax on his crop down the road.

It's important not to be fooled by investments that masquerade as tax-free, like municipal bonds. Municipal bonds may be, in fact, federal-tax-free, but unless you purchase them from the state you live in, they may not be state-tax-free. And if they gain value (not just interest) due to fluctuations in interest rates, you also have to pay tax on this gain. Municipal bonds should be considered tax-efficient in some cases, but not tax-free.

PROVISIONAL INCOME

Another important concept to understand is provisional income. This is the type of income the IRS counts when determining how to tax you on certain things. To be truly tax-free, an investment needs to provide income that cannot count as provisional income. This is income included in the calculation of Social Security tax or Medicare premium adjustments. Municipal bond interest does not fit this bill, as it is considered provisional income. We will discuss more about provisional income later in the book.

Remember, the key is to understand which bucket an account fits into before you decide where to put your hard-earned money. The "tax me now" bucket commonly includes bank accounts, mutual funds, and brokerage accounts and is useful for liquidity and short-term savings. The "tax me later" bucket is the most popular—and least beneficial—for retirement savings, and we will discuss this in more detail later. The "tax me never" bucket is very important and underutilized. Most people do not understand all the benefits investments in this bucket can have on their future. They are unaware of the compounding tax time bombs they are creating by not contributing more to this bucket.

It is important to determine your ideal number, as we will discuss later, for the tax-deferred bucket and not to exceed it. You should then consider strategies that allow you to shift money to, and accumulate most of your retirement savings in, the tax-free bucket. Keep reading to learn why and how to take advantage of the "tax me never" bucket, no matter what your circumstances may be.

Chapter 3

ARE YOU BORROWING MONEY FROM THE IRS?

Are you contributing to a tax-deferred plan (a "tax me later" account), like a traditional IRA or 401(k), as a way to save for retirement? Millions of Americans do this every payday. These types of accounts are by far the most popular ones Americans use to save for retirement. That doesn't make them the best choice in all circumstances, though.

Do you realize you're taking a small loan from the IRS each time you contribute to your IRA or 401(k)? If you didn't know this or you don't want to borrow from the IRS and have the burden of a tax lien on your retirement accounts in the future, keep reading.

YOUR TAX DEDUCTIONS ARE REALLY A LOAN

Here's a secret: those tax "deductions" you take today aren't truly deductions. They are an advance on your retirement savings that you'll repay someday, and then some. In short, it's basically a loan you take from the IRS each pay period that you will have to repay when you retire—a time in your life when you need the most money possible.

When you contribute $100 from your paycheck into your IRA or traditional 401(k) plan, you aren't really saving a full $100. The $100 is pre-tax money and was never all yours to begin with. The IRS was always going to take its tax from that pay. But by putting the $100 into your traditional 401(k), the IRS has given you a pass on paying that tax—for now. By giving you a tax deduction this year, the IRS instantly has a lien on that $100 for all the taxes you will owe on it one day, at whatever the tax rates will be when you take it out.

Let's take a look at an example.

For simplicity, let's say you are in a 20 percent tax bracket. When you save that $100 into your 401(k), pre-tax, you reduce your taxes that pay period by $20. That's an extra $20 in your pocket for you to spend! But what you really did was save $80 of that $100 and took a small loan of $20 from the IRS that you have to pay back later in life.

Later, when you take out your $100 during retirement, you

will owe back the tax deduction (loan) and probably more, if you consider the growth. If your $100 grows to $200, you will owe taxes on twice the amount of your original deduction. That's like paying interest on the small $20 loan you originally took. So what should you do?

AN EASY WAY TO BOOST YOUR RETIREMENT SAVINGS

Understanding that tax deductions on your retirement money are a loan from the IRS offers you an easy way to boost your retirement savings. This is great news, as it's no secret Americans aren't so good at saving for the future. In fact, we have one of the lowest savings rates in the world compared to other developed countries. So let's look at how you can boost your savings by making a simple change to something you're probably already doing: contributing to your 401(k) at work.

More than 70 percent of retirement plans in America now offer a Roth 401(k) option, yet very few people contribute to it. There are a couple of reasons for this. First, the Roth option hasn't been around that long compared to the Traditional 401(k) option. Roth was introduced in 1997, but it wasn't until recently that many employers added the Roth option to their workplace retirement plans. Second, when it was added to plans, most people didn't bother to switch their contributions over to it. This could be because they were lazy and thought it was too much hassle, they didn't understand the choice, or didn't think it would benefit them to switch. From my experience in working with savers over the years, I find the latter is usually the case. People didn't fully understand the benefit of tax-free growth and instead opted to continue receiving the tax deductions (loans) from the IRS. They believed it would be better to take the deductions now and maybe pay them back later in life, when they thought they might be in a lower tax bracket. We'll explore why this is a myth in the next chapter.

So one reason you should consider switching to the Roth option is because it is the easiest way to boost your retirement savings and help "future you." Some worry that by stopping contributions to their traditional 401(k) or switching to the Roth option, they will lose out on tax deductions. This is true, but you have to remember...

> The point of your retirement account is not to give you a tax deduction. It's to maximize your income at a point in life when you need your money the most—in retirement.

By switching to the Roth 401(k) option, you will actually be saving the full $100 every pay period toward your future, and the money will be tax-free, not just tax-deferred! It's true the money you take home will decrease by the $20 you were borrowing from the IRS, but wouldn't you rather sacrifice that meager $20 now and have a retirement account that is *all* yours one day, instead of partially owned by the IRS?

Some would argue that if you use the traditional plan and save the tax deduction as well, you could have even more money down the road by utilizing tax-deferred accounts. This is true in certain circumstances, but the problem with this argument is that I have rarely met anyone who actually saves the tax deduction they receive each pay period. Do you calculate this and put the money aside every two weeks? You probably don't. Nobody really does this, which is why it's not an effective strategy. When you instead switch to the Roth 401(k), you put away the money you were receiving as a tax deduction (loan). It's easy, and it's all done for you. The argument of saving the tax deduction also doesn't take into account the tax consequences of where you might save that extra money in your "tax me now" bucket (like a brokerage, mutual fund, or bank account) or other taxes that may be triggered annually, as you will learn later in this book.

If you don't have access to a Roth 401(k) option at work, then consider lowering the contributions to your traditional 401(k) to the minimum amount required to receive the company match, if there is one. Many employers will match (or contribute extra money to) your workplace retirement plan if you contribute a certain amount—usually a percentage of your salary. The match is free money from your employer, so you should take advantage of it.

You should contribute to a regular Roth IRA beyond the

amount that is matched. If you are still able to save more after you have maxed out this account, consider a regular brokerage account or the mega-backdoor Roth strategy discussed later in this book. If you really have a lot to save, you can also consider a Life Insurance Retirement Plan (LIRP), which is also discussed later in this book.

Also, it's important to have *some* money in the tax-deferred bucket upon reaching retirement. We will explore the reasons why and how much you should have (your ideal number) later.

THE CRIME AGAINST YOUNG PEOPLE

One of the biggest crimes in America is happening to younger people across the country, and it is sad to witness. I call it a crime because this issue will literally rob millions from the younger generations over time, to the benefit of the IRS. Too many people are starting their careers today without being educated on the benefits of the Roth IRA and Roth 401(k). They are being told (by older generations, mostly) to start contributing their money to tax-deferred plans, like the traditional 401(k). Not many young people are good at saving money, but for those who are, it's a shame how many of them start with contributions to tax-deferred plans—especially when they're probably in the lowest income tax bracket they will ever be in!

When someone starts their first real job in life, they usually earn the least amount of money they will ever make. Think back to your first job and how much money you made. It seemed pretty great at the time, but can you imagine living on that money now? Probably not. And I will bet you were in a lower tax bracket back in those days as well. Why would a young person want to save on taxes (or more accurately, put them off until later) when they are only paying 10 or maybe 12 percent in taxes? As a single person, you can earn up to $53,075 in America in 2021 and still be in the 12 percent marginal tax bracket. Also in 2021, married couples stay in the 12 percent tax bracket until their combined earnings reach $106,150. This encompasses most people and their first salary in life.

AN EXAMPLE

Travis just got his first real job out of college. The company offered him a starting salary of $55,000 for his first year, and he couldn't be more excited. He wants to do everything right, so he signs up for the traditional 401(k) his new company offers on the recommendation of his parents. He reads the conventional wisdom that he should put 10 percent of his salary away for retirement and decides that is what he will do. This gets him $5,500 in pre-tax contributions his first year.

Since Travis only has $36,950 of taxable income (his $55,000 salary minus $5,500 401(k) contribution minus the $12,550 standard deduction), he is only in the 12 percent tax bracket. Thus, his contributions to his traditional 401(k) only saved him $660 in his first year at work ($55 a month). And now that he's taken that small deduction (loan) from the IRS, he's committed to paying it back at some future time, possibly with penalties, at an unknown tax rate that will probably be much higher than the 12 percent he pays now. He will also be committed to paying taxes on every penny of growth that money makes and compounds over his entire working career, as well!

Young people need to learn more about how the IRS and taxes work and create better plans. They need to start contributing to the Roth 401(k) or Roth IRA when they are young and the minuscule tax savings from pre-tax accounts don't do much for them. This will allow them to avoid the tax time bombs you will learn about in this book, and avoid lighting the fuse at such an early age! If you know someone who is just starting out in their career, share this book with them. Or once you have finished this book, sit down with that young person and teach them why they need to keep their money from the IRS. This would benefit younger people and make the world a better place for them.

If you don't want to borrow from the IRS each pay period and create a tax lien on your future, consider shifting your savings to the "tax-free" bucket using strategies we will discuss shortly. If you don't have an adequate emergency fund already, shift your savings to meet this goal first, and once accomplished, pay off any high-interest debt (credit cards) before shifting to tax-free savings. When you contribute to this bucket, you will actually save the full $100. You will avoid falling victim to this country's crime against young people and create a strong foundation for a tax-free retirement.

Chapter 4

WHY YOU SHOULDN'T TAKE ADVICE FROM YOUR TAX PREPARER

I don't have anything against tax preparers. They are a necessity in our world where everything seems to have become so complex, you need a specialist to help. But I urge you to understand how most tax preparers think and why this thought process is usually not in your best interest. Many are not even aware of the harm they cause. They have just never been taught to think about taxes holistically.

Some tax preparers are also tax planners, but this is rare. It's a small distinction, but one that can make a big difference. It is best to work with your fiduciary financial advisor (who is also a tax planner and preferably a tax-free planning specialist) on tax planning issues and then take that advice to your tax preparer for them to execute. Let's discuss why.

The tax preparation industry seems to have one goal each and every year: to help you receive the largest refund legally possible on your tax return. Notice I did not say their goal is to help you pay the least amount of taxes. Your tax preparer may make this claim as well, but the question is one of time frames. They rarely consider that the largest refund might not be in your overall best interest. It is like going to a restaurant that believes you are only there to eat the most food possible. They will promise to help you get the absolute most food into your stomach, regardless of the health consequences to you!

Tax people tend to think in terms of the biggest refund in the current tax year and nothing else. They understand most people feel happiest when they receive the largest possible amount of money back from their tax return. Tax preparation is a business, and it's good business to make your customers happy, right? How else would they expect to get referrals and repeat business? Here's another secret:

Getting the most back from your tax return each year may not be in your best interest when considering your *lifetime* tax plan. Most tax preparers consider a single tax year but never your lifetime tax plan.

Would you take a loan from me today if I said you had to pay it back quadruple later? That is, with 400 percent interest? Maybe you would, but in most cases I think you'd agree it wouldn't be in your best interest to pay so much interest. Yet that is exactly what so many people do when they maximize their retirement plan deductions for the current year. They are just kicking the tax issue (payments) down the road, with a compounding effect they don't think about. Many Americans will happily push off the problem until later, not realizing that putting off the problem isn't like kicking a can down the road. It's more like pushing a wet snowball down a snowy slope!

THE INSTANT GRATIFICATION ISSUE

This problem of instant gratification in America isn't new. It is pervasive throughout our culture and only appears to be getting worse. It rears its ugly head everywhere and can be damaging when left unchecked. From the overuse of credit cards to sign-and-drive programs to needing your Amazon delivery within two hours, this mindset is financially devastating, especially when it comes to your taxes.

The most financial damage from the instant gratification craze happens when Americans want a little more from their tax return and are willing to sacrifice their future income substantially to have it now, as you will see in upcoming examples. It is even worse when they take a tax refund loan from their tax preparer with a high interest rate and a service fee built right into it. For example, someone could receive a $2,000 refund in two to three weeks, but they'll gladly accept a $1,500 refund loan today instead of waiting. It's as if people have to have everything now!

INSTANT GRATIFICATION IN FINANCE

Unfortunately, advice based on instant gratification bleeds into the financial industry as well. Too many financial advisors are happy to tell you to contribute to an IRA and save on your taxes this year. This is the easiest, laziest advice to give, and it's usually bad advice. Most do so without ever putting any thought into the future tax rates you may be subject to or future tax time bombs—this advice may light the fuse. They do so without any comprehensive tax or financial plan in place for you. Here is a very important point...

> If your financial advisor hasn't discussed taxes as part of your financial or investment plan or asked to see your last tax return, this is a sign you should seek a new advisor. A true financial plan (or planner) cannot exist without considering your current *and* lifetime taxes.

Many financial salespeople are also eager to sell tax-deferred investment products, like annuities. These products often pay salespeople very large upfront commissions and come with long surrender periods (a period of time when you cannot get your money out without penalties). They are products that, when structured incorrectly, can compound your tax problems later in life. The salespeople pushing these products convince you that you can keep more money from the IRS if you just buy tax-deferred products and don't run the risk of pushing yourself into a higher tax bracket. Not all financial salespeople are bad, and neither are all annuities. Just be careful when considering both.

However, it's not just the nonfiduciary financial salesperson gaming the American public. The system created by the IRS is an even more elaborate tax maze full of trickery and misconceptions. Many tax regulations are designed to put more money in the coffers of the IRS at your expense. You will understand how they do this after reading the next section of this book. But before we get into how to beat the IRS, let's discuss the biggest myth (and argument) surrounding tax-deferred investing: being in a lower tax bracket during retirement means tax-deferred investments are good.

Chapter 5

THE MYTH OF LOWER TAX BRACKETS IN RETIREMENT

When I talk to people about the benefits of switching their retirement savings from the traditional IRA and 401(k) to the Roth IRA and Roth 401(k), or why they probably don't want the biggest tax refund possible this year, I hear the same argument almost every time:

"I'm going to be in a lower tax bracket in retirement, right? Doesn't it make sense to get the tax break now and pay taxes at a lower rate in retirement?"

In this chapter, we will discuss this argument and examine examples with numbers to see what saving and withdrawing in retirement could actually look like. We will also see some of the tax time bombs in action.

First, let me address this common argument. If you have saved and planned properly for retirement, you might not be in a lower tax bracket, especially if tax rates increase between now and when you withdraw your money in retirement. And even if you are in a lower tax bracket in retirement, it probably won't be *low enough* to save you anything in the long run, as you will see.

When you put your money into a tax-deferred plan to save money this year, you won't just owe taxes down the road on what you saved. You will also owe taxes on the growth of that money (as we'll learn more about with Tax Time Bomb 3). The IRS has a lien on your *entire* account for those taxes, and they will collect!

SAVING FOR RETIREMENT

Let's assume you make $120,000 per year. That puts you squarely in the 24 percent marginal tax bracket for 2021 tax rates. You want to save for retirement, so you contribute $19,000 a year into your traditional 401(k) at work. (The maximum allowable contribution in 2021 is actually $19,500, but to keep things simple, we will assume an even $19,000). This saves you $4,560 in taxes each year, and you have a little extra in your paycheck every two weeks. You probably just spend that little extra from every paycheck, so it has no real benefit to your future. And you will owe taxes on the entire balance in your 401(k) account someday. Now let's fast forward.

You do this every year for thirty years, and along the way, your investments earn an average of 8 percent. For simplicity in this illustration, we will assume you never get a raise and the amount you contribute never changes either. Plus, you don't get any match from your employer. Here is a simple table showing how your account would grow over time:

Year	Start Balance	Interest	End Balance
1	$0.00	$0.00	$19,000.00
2	$19,000.00	$1,520.00	$39,520.00
3	$39,520.00	$3,161.60	$61,681.60
4	$61,681.60	$4,934.53	$85,616.13
5	$85,616.13	$6,849.29	$111,465.42
6	$111,465.42	$8,917.23	$139,382.65
7	$139,382.65	$11,150.61	$169,533.26
8	$169,533.26	$13,562.66	$202,095.92
9	$202,095.92	$16,167.67	$237,263.60
10	$237,263.60	$18,981.09	$275,244.69
11	$275,244.69	$22,019.57	$316,264.26
12	$316,264.26	$25,301.14	$360,565.40
13	$360,565.40	$28,845.23	$408,410.63
14	$408,410.63	$32,672.85	$460,083.49
15	$460,083.49	$36,806.68	$515,890.16
16	$515,890.16	$41,271.21	$576,161.38
17	$576,161.38	$46,092.91	$641,254.29
18	$641,254.29	$51,300.34	$711,554.63
19	$711,554.63	$56,924.37	$787,479.00
20	$787,479.00	$62,998.32	$869,477.32
21	$869,477.32	$69,558.19	$958,035.51
22	$958,035.51	$76,642.84	$1,053,678.35
23	$1,053,678.35	$84,294.27	$1,156,972.62
24	$1,156,972.62	$92,557.81	$1,268,530.43
25	$1,268,530.43	$101,482.43	$1,389,012.86
26	$1,389,012.86	$111,121.03	$1,519,133.89
27	$1,519,133.89	$121,530.71	$1,659,664.60
28	$1,659,664.60	$132,773.17	$1,811,437.77
29	$1,811,437.77	$144,915.02	$1,975,352.79
30	$1,975,352.79	$158,028.22	**$2,152,381.01**

At the end of thirty years, you would have over $2,150,000 in your 401(k), and if you add up your tax savings ($4,560 times thirty years), you'd have $136,800 in total tax savings. Not bad, and most people would love to keep this much money from the IRS, as well as have a 401(k) balance like this one! The problem is, you haven't kept anything from the IRS. You have simply *delayed* giving it to them. The instant gratification of $4,560 more in a tax refund each year (as a loan from the IRS) will catch up to you.

WITHDRAWING FOR RETIREMENT

Let's assume now, after thirty years of working, you would like to retire. For simplicity, let's also assume you are now old enough (59.5 years or older) to not have any withdrawal penalties on top of the taxes you will owe, which we will discuss in Tax Time Bomb 2. I imagine you wouldn't take all of your money from this account on the first day of retirement. If you did, it would incur a whopping tax bill! I am also going to assume you follow the widely recognized 4 percent rule and withdraw 4 percent of your account balance each year for income, with a 3 percent raise each year for inflation. For more information on the 4 percent rule, visit the Resources page at Divorce-The-IRS.com.

Following this rule, in the first year of retirement, you would take $86,095 from your account. This would put you in a lower marginal tax bracket in retirement—if this was your only source of income. You would be in the 22 percent marginal tax bracket, based on rates for 2021, and have an effective rate of 14.07 percent. This means you would pay $12,115 in federal tax on your withdrawal (plus state income tax in most states).

In your second year of retirement, you would take $88,678 from your account ($86,095 plus 3 percent raise for inflation). This would keep you in the 22 percent marginal bracket and give you a 14.3 percent effective tax rate. You would pay $12,684 in federal taxes. Let's compound this over a thirty-year retirement.

Year	Withdrawal	Taxes	Marginal Bracket	Effective Tax Rate
1	$86,095.00	$12,115.00	22.00%	14.07%
2	$88,677.85	$12,684.00	22.00%	14.30%
3	$91,338.19	$13,269.00	22.00%	14.53%
4	$94,078.33	$13,872.00	22.00%	14.74%
5	$96,900.68	$14,503.00	24.00%	14.97%
6	$99,807.70	$15,200.00	24.00%	15.23%
7	$102,801.93	$15,919.00	24.00%	15.49%
8	$105,885.99	$16,659.00	24.00%	15.73%
9	$109,062.57	$17,421.00	24.00%	15.97%
10	$112,334.45	$18,207.00	24.00%	16.21%
11	$115,704.48	$19,015.00	24.00%	16.43%
12	$119,175.62	$19,849.00	24.00%	16.65%
13	$122,750.88	$20,707.00	24.00%	16.87%
14	$126,433.41	$21,590.00	24.00%	17.08%
15	$130,226.41	$22,501.00	24.00%	17.28%
16	$134,133.20	$23,438.00	24.00%	17.47%
17	$138,157.20	$24,404.00	24.00%	17.66%
18	$142,301.92	$25,399.00	24.00%	17.85%
19	$146,570.97	$26,423.00	24.00%	18.03%
20	$150,968.10	$27,479.00	24.00%	18.20%
21	$155,497.15	$28,566.00	24.00%	18.37%
22	$160,162.06	$29,685.00	24.00%	18.53%
23	$164,966.92	$30,838.00	24.00%	18.69%
24	$169,915.93	$32,026.00	24.00%	18.85%
25	$175,013.41	$33,417.00	32.00%	19.09%
26	$180,263.81	$35,097.00	32.00%	19.47%
27	$185,671.73	$36,827.00	32.00%	19.83%
28	$191,241.88	$38,610.00	32.00%	20.19%
29	$196,979.13	$40,446.00	32.00%	20.53%
30	$202,888.51	$42,337.00	32.00%	20.87%
Totals	**$4,096,005.42**	**$728,503.00**		

As you can see in the chart, you would end up paying $728,503 in taxes over the thirty years of your retirement!

Would you like $138,600 in savings over your thirty-year career just so you can pay back the IRS $728,503 in retirement?

Even though you took all your tax deductions while you were working at the full 24 percent savings rate and paid taxes back in retirement with a much lower effective tax rate, it still didn't work out for you. Not even close. It worked out really well for the IRS, though!

Saving while in a higher tax bracket probably will not benefit you down the road. It doesn't matter that you will be in a lower bracket later—this is a myth. Even if you do end up in a lower tax bracket, you probably won't be in a low enough bracket to ever save a penny on taxes due to the growth of the tax-deferred account (and thus the tax on it). The only way to pay less in taxes during retirement is to follow the advice in this book early in life and make smart choices now so you can achieve a 0 percent (or very near 0 percent) tax bracket in retirement. Let's look at a couple more scenarios using this example to further illustrate the point.

SOME OTHER SCENARIOS

Maybe you don't believe you will earn 8 percent on your investments over time. Maybe you are more conservative than that. Maybe you don't think it's sustainable to take 4 percent out for income every year *and* give yourself a 3 percent raise. Let's take a look at what happens in each of these scenarios as well to make sure you completely understand why this is a myth.

Imagine you didn't take a raise every year of your retirement and instead just took a level income of $86,095 per year. You would only pay $12,115 a year (every year) in taxes at an effective rate of 14.07 percent (assuming tax rates never increased). Even in this scenario, you would still end up paying the IRS $363,450 in taxes over the course of your retirement. That is more than double what you saved while working.

Let's say you were more conservative and only earned 6 percent average on your money while saving for retirement. You would end up with an IRA balance of $1,502,105 instead of over $2,150,000. Taking out 4 percent each year and never giving yourself a raise would mean $60,084 of taxable income each year. You would owe $6,393 of federal tax per year on this income (22 percent marginal and 10.64 percent effective rates). Multiply that by thirty years, and you'd pay back $191,790 in taxes to the IRS for your $136,000 in tax savings. It still did not work out in your best interest.

And this just considers federal tax. The effect is compounded if you happen to live in a state that has state income tax as well (and forty-three of the fifty states do).

What if you expect to have other retirement income as well? Most retirees will have other sources of income from things like their taxable bucket, rental income, and Social Security. Add all of this to your income, and you can see how you probably won't be in a lower tax bracket (or pay less tax) in retirement.

THE TRUTH OF THE MYTH

For those who save in life, which is hopefully you, there just isn't any way to be in a low enough tax bracket in retirement to avoid paying *more* taxes back than you saved with tax-deferred investing. Nothing will stop the IRS from collecting that tax, either. Even if you pass away, your beneficiaries will have to pay all that tax, and probably more (see Tax Time Bomb 7).

On top of that, the money you withdraw in retirement from your tax-deferred accounts has the potential to make your Social Security taxable (Tax Time Bomb 3) and increase your Medicare premiums, as well (Tax Time Bomb 4). See the Resources page at Divorce-The-IRS.com for more details on the impact taxes have on Social Security.

When you factor those taxes into the equation, along with the fact that current tax rates are set to expire in 2025 and then increase (Tax Time Bomb 1), you will probably end up paying even more taxes in retirement than you realize!

As we talk about the complications involved in saving and withdrawing for retirement, you begin to see there are many tax time bombs to consider to effectively divorce the IRS and avoid paying them more tax than necessary. Specifically, there are eight tax time bombs which can help you avoid falling for myths like the one in this chapter and other myths which we'll explore in this book. Now let's discuss these tax time bombs and how you can defuse them.

Part II

TAX TIME BOMBS

Chapter 6

TAX TIME BOMB 1

EXPLODING TAX RATES

Now that we've discussed some basic tax concepts, you have the knowledge to understand the biggest tax time bombs—the ones with the potential to destroy your retirement savings. There are eight of them, and they can explode at various stages of a person's journey toward or throughout retirement. In this part of the book, Part 2, we will cover these time bombs and the strategies to avoid them. You may have escaped or already experienced some of these situations. If not, you can avoid most of them with proper, comprehensive financial planning, especially if you start early in life. This is something within our control, and we will go into the details of these strategies in Part 3.

However, some factors in life that affect financial planning are completely out of our control, and we can only speculate as to what may happen in those circumstances. That brings us to the first tax time bomb: exploding tax rates.

One of the circumstances we have no control over is the tax rates in America. Much has been written about the state of the current US deficit, as well as the problems with Social Security and Medicare. We don't need to enter into that discussion in this book, except to say the current government deficit is over $26 trillion. It's out of control, and both Social Security and Medicare will need a lot of funding help in the future. There are only two ways to help with these problems: cut government spending (which is hard for anyone and seems impossible for the government) and/or raise taxes.

If you haven't already, I encourage you to take a brief history lesson on tax rates in the United States, which you can find on the Resources page at Divorce-The-IRS.com. Most people are amazed to realize that not long ago, in the 1980s, the top marginal tax rate was 50 percent. In the 1970s, it was 70 percent. In the '60s, it was as high as 91 percent! Today, the top marginal bracket is only 37 percent.

We currently have historically low tax rates which are set to expire at the end of 2025. Assuming there is no further tax legislation between now and then, tax rates will revert back to the pre-Tax Cut and Jobs Act rates. This means income tax brackets will rise across most income levels.

I am the first to admit that I don't have a crystal ball, but I think it's fair (and fun) to guess the future of taxes. As I write, the government is spending like never before due to the COVID-19 pandemic, and the national deficit is ballooning. I think it's a fair assumption to guess that tax rates will likely increase from here. And if that's the case, there is currently an opportunity we may never see again in our lifetimes to utilize Roth strategies and conversions in financial planning. In other words, we have the chance to pay all the taxes possible now at known and historically low rates so you won't have to pay taxes later at unknown future rates.

DEFUSE THIS BOMB BY PAYING TAXES NOW

When I suggest to people that they should pay more taxes now *on purpose* because we have known and very low tax rates, they usually balk at me! But people rush to take advantage of this concept in another area of financial life we are all familiar with: mortgages. Currently, we are also experiencing historically low mortgage interest rates. I don't know of a single homeowner who wouldn't like to refinance their home (usually extending their mortgage out to thirty years again) to take advantage of known and historically low interest rates. They rush out and pay all sorts of refinancing fees to lock in that known rate for the next thirty years! This is exactly the same as what I am suggesting you consider with your tax-deferred money and current savings by utilizing a Roth conversion. Consider it refinancing your IRA.

Most of the tax time bombs people are building and holding now will only get worse and create an even bigger negative explosion should tax rates rise from here. Just a 1 or 2 percent rise in taxes can have a *massive* compounding effect later in life. If you are saving and getting today's tax bracket deductions just to pay taxes on that same money plus its growth down the road at higher rates, you obviously haven't done yourself any favors. Uncle Sam and the IRS will sure love you, though.

I understand why people balk at the idea of paying all possible taxes now instead of delaying the pain. However, you will have to pay those taxes at some point, and taking advantage of the current, historically low rates means you will likely give considerably less to the IRS in your lifetime. It's a wise way to defuse the tax time bomb of exploding tax rates, which are out of our control.

This leads us to the effects of another early action you may take: early withdrawal of your retirement savings. As we'll discover in the next chapter, this is a time bomb which carries serious penalties.

Chapter 7

TAX TIME BOMB 2

EARLY WITHDRAWAL PENALTIES

If you are like most people, it's likely that life will throw you a monkey wrench some time before you reach retirement. It's probably already happened—many times over, maybe. Life is constantly throwing us curveballs!

When this happens, people often need money to rectify a situation, whether it be a divorce, a costly repair to a vehicle or home, or something else. Unfortunately, one place people turn to fund these expenses is their retirement savings—the money they put away into tax-deferred plans like an IRA or their 401(k) at work.

When you deposited money into these plans, you realized a tax deduction (or, as you learned earlier, you borrowed a little money from the IRS). Now that life has happened and you need that money before the age of 59.5 years, the IRS will collect on that loan, and then some.

AN EARLY WITHDRAWAL EXAMPLE

Let's take a thirty-five-year-old, Mike, who makes around $100,000 a year of taxable income. This means he is in the 24 percent federal tax bracket. And while every state differs, let's estimate a 6 percent state tax rate for this example.

Mike had a big life event and needs $30,000. He is considering taking this money from his 401(k) at work. Assuming he wants to take all funds and expenses from his 401(k) to actually net $30,000 in his pocket, he would have to withdraw $50,000. Why so much? Let's break it down:

$50,000 total withdrawal

– $12,000 federal taxes due

– $5,000 early withdrawal penalty at 10 percent

– $3,000 state taxes due

= $30,000 net to Mike

This is the first tax time bomb explosion that many Americans face in life, when they have no choice but to take money out of their tax-deferred retirement plan before reaching retirement age. Upon doing this, they owe back the tax deduction (loan) they once received on their contributions. Often, they owe even more if the withdrawal pushes them into a higher tax bracket. And, to add insult to injury, they have to pay an *additional* 10 percent penalty on the money they withdrew.

It's one thing if a big life event happens unexpectedly and you have absolutely no other place to withdraw money from. It amazes me how often, though, I see people take money out in this way for nonemergency purposes, like to pay for a wedding or to purchase a new car or boat. It's like watching someone stare at a grenade in their hand after they just pulled the pin. It's stupid.

To make matters worse, you also have to consider the future value of the money that was withdrawn. Had Mike left that $50,000 in his retirement account and realized an average 8 percent return until he was sixty years old, he would have had a little over $342,000. That's quite a bit to give up for $30,000 in his pocket today! This is an explosion that doesn't just hurt immediately when he pays the tax and penalty—it continues to hurt with the regret of knowing he really took out $342,000 worth of future retirement happiness.

DEFUSE THIS BOMB WITH AN EMERGENCY FUND AND ROTH ACCOUNTS

One of the easiest ways to avoid this painful tax explosion

is to have a proper emergency fund. Any fiduciary financial planner's first piece of advice is to establish three to six months' worth of living expenses in a liquid savings account or non-qualified investment account (taxable bucket) as an emergency fund.

If you follow the advice in this book, you will have an emergency fund to fall back on. But if you need more money than what that can provide and you put your retirement money in Roth accounts as this book advises, you will also be able to access all the contributions you made to the Roth account without taxes or penalties.

It is only the growth in a Roth account you have to pay tax and the 10 percent early withdrawal penalty on, if withdrawn prior to age 59.5. It still hurts to withdraw that money, as once it has been out of the account for more than sixty days, its fate is sealed, and you cannot replace that money or its future tax-free value. However, you will have avoided the explosive effects of most early withdrawal penalties.

Another advisor once shared with me the advice she gives clients when they ask if they can afford something, and it's stuck with me over the years. She said, "If you can't afford to buy it twice, you can't afford it." If you live by this motto while making all purchases in life, you won't end up withdrawing your savings early. You will do all right.

Chapter 8

TAX TIME BOMB 3

SHARING YOUR RETIREMENT WITH THE IRS

Imagine you have now made it to retirement. Congratulations! This is a big milestone in a person's life, as well as a big transition. You have worked for decades, saving money and doing without, and it's time to relax a little and enjoy the fruits of your labor. The problem is, the IRS is just as ready to enjoy the fruits of your labor!

Now that you are ready to receive income from your tax-deferred accounts, like your IRA and 401(k), the IRS is ready to take their share. They will start collecting on all those little loans they gave you over the years in the form of tax deductions. There isn't a single penny in your tax-deferred accounts that won't be taxed!

You may realize you don't seem to be in a lower marginal tax bracket like you expected. Wasn't that the plan all along, to be in a lower tax bracket in retirement and not pay as much tax? Since you planned and saved well, you have almost the same income now as when you were working. Your effective tax rate may be a bit lower now, but not enough to significantly reduce your overall tax bill. Maybe tax rates have increased as well.

You no longer have any of those tax deductions or credits you once enjoyed. There are no more pre-tax contributions to retirement accounts or health savings accounts and no mortgage interest deduction (hopefully). The children's tax credits left the same time they did, and student loan interest deductions are probably also long gone at this point.

You realize that the $1 million IRA you worked so hard to build is only about 80 percent yours. That's right—it may say you have $1 million, but in reality, the IRS has a lien on that account for about 20 percent, and maybe more. Just jump back to the earlier example in which we discussed the myth of the lower tax bracket in retirement. You will see that 20 percent of that beautiful 401(k) balance was actually the property of the IRS. This tax time bomb is hard to swallow.

Take a look at your current IRA or 401(k) balance. I'm sure it's not as much as you would like to have (it never is), but you are proud of that balance. You worked hard to save that money. Now imagine 20 percent of it gone. How does that make you feel? That is the reality of your account. Only about 80 percent of the balance is actually yours. The rest belongs to the IRS.

DEFUSE THIS BOMB BY KNOWING YOUR NUMBER

Not all tax-deferred money is bad, and this strategy definitely has its place in financial planning. But working with a good fiduciary financial planner earlier in life would have revealed there is a very specific amount of money you want to have in your tax-deferred bucket upon reaching retirement. This number would have allowed you to achieve a 0 percent tax bracket during retirement, even with money in tax-deferred accounts. I call this your ideal number.

We will discuss this amount and the strategies surrounding it after we get through the rest of the tax time bombs. For now, understand that effectively saving for retirement is not about putting as much money as possible into tax-deferred accounts like your IRA and 401(k). You need to calculate your ideal number and create a plan to achieve it, so you don't lose 20 percent of your retirement savings to the IRS.

And if you think that is the only way the IRS taxes you during retirement, get ready for another tax time bomb explosion!

Chapter 9

TAX TIME BOMB 4

SOCIAL SECURITY TAX

Let's stick with the idea that you are now retired. You've come to terms with the realization that you only own about 80 percent of your tax-deferred retirement accounts and that you are now in a partnership for life with the IRS. You are reluctantly paying taxes on everything you take out of those accounts as income, and it's a lot more than you ever thought a retiree would pay.

Now it's time to boost your retirement income with Social Security. You won't have to rely so heavily on your own retirement accounts, and maybe it can help you pay less tax. You paid into the system for all those years with taxes, right? It's time for it to pay off.

However, when you got your first Social Security check, you weren't counting on another tax time bomb going off! That's right—you built this benefit throughout your career by paying *a lot* of taxes for it, and now the IRS is going to tax your benefit.

Depending on whether you are single or married, there is a limit on the amount of provisional income you can take during retirement before your Social Security gets taxed. This means if you take money that is considered provisional income, it will be included in a calculation to determine how much, if any, tax you will owe on your Social Security income. Provisional income generally includes:

1. Half of your Social Security income.
2. Any distributions from your tax-deferred bucket (such as IRAs and 401(k)s).
3. Interest or growth from your "tax me now" bucket investments, reported on your 1099 forms (such as CDs and savings accounts at your bank).
4. Income from any employment.
5. Interest and capital gains from municipal bonds.
6. All rental income.

The IRS will add all of this up, and if you are over the thresholds set by the IRS, you will be taxed on your Social Security at your highest marginal tax rate. The thresholds are not that high, either.

HOW TAX ON SOCIAL SECURITY WORKS

If you are single and your provisional income is greater than $25,000 in 2021, you will owe taxes on your Social Security. Married couples start paying taxes on Social Security once their combined provisional income reaches $32,000. You can find an online calculator to help determine how much Social Security tax you may owe, and there is a link is on the Resources page at Divorce-The-IRS.com. This table shows how these calculations are determined. They can add up to a lot more than people realize.

Taxable portions of income for Social Security beneficiaries, by income tax filing status and modified AGI

Line	Modified AGI (nominal $)	Taxable portion of income
	Single	
1	Less than 25,000	None
2	25,000–34,000	Lesser of— • 50 percent of benefit income; or • modified AGI in excess of $25,000
3	More than 34,000	Lesser of— • 85 percent of benefit income; or • amount from line 2 plus 85 percent of modified AGI in excess of $34,000
	Married, filing jointly	
4	Less than 32,000	None
5	32,000–44,000	Lesser of— • 50 percent of benefit income; or • modified AGI in excess of $32,000
6	More than 44,000	Lesser of— • 85 percent of benefit income; or • amount from line 5 plus 85 percent of modified AGI in excess of $44,000

SOURCE: IRS (2015b)
NOTE: Modified AGI is AGI plus nontaxable interest income plus income from foreign sources

A SOCIAL SECURITY TAX EXAMPLE

Bill and Sally have a combined Social Security income of $30,000. In order to meet their lifestyle needs, they would like to take an additional $80,000 from their IRAs. To figure out their provisional income, we take half of their Social Security ($15,000) and add it to the $80,000 they withdraw from their IRAs. This makes Bill and Sally's provisional income $95,000, and because this is over the maximum threshold of $44,000 for married couples, they now owe taxes on 85 percent of their Social Security income at their highest marginal tax rate.

Thus, 85 percent of their $30,000 of Social Security is $25,500. This is piled right on top of their other income (IRA withdrawal of $80,000) and taxed at 22 percent (the 2021 tax rate). Bill and Sally would owe $5,610 of tax on just their Social Security, simply because they took too much out of their IRAs.

DEFUSE THIS BOMB BY CONSIDERING PROVISIONAL INCOME

See the Resources page at Divorce-The-IRS.com for more details about tax on Social Security and how provisional income works. This is yet another tax explosion that is preventable with comprehensive financial planning and the utilization of tax-free strategies earlier in life.

You see, the money you withdraw from tax-free accounts

isn't just tax-free; it isn't included in the calculation that can make your Social Security taxable. In other words, it isn't considered provisional income. So you are able to take as much income from a tax-free account as you'd like without ever worrying about making your Social Security taxable and exploding this tax time bomb on yourself. Once you're aware of this, you can consider another tax that most people don't think of: Medicare premiums.

Chapter 10

TAX TIME BOMB 5

MEDICARE PREMIUMS

For some people, the tax time bombs just keep going off! Medicare premium surcharges are another tax people don't think about until they have to pay it.

Healthcare in retirement is widely misunderstood. The Nationwide Retirement Institute's *Fourth Annual Health Care and Long-Term Care Survey* found that 72 percent of adults over age fifty admit they don't fully understand how Medicare works, and more than half believe coverage is free.

Medicare is far from free, and the premiums increase with income, a lot like Social Security tax. At certain thresholds, you will have to pay higher Medicare Part B and D premiums.

HOW MEDICARE PREMIUMS WORK

This tax, or extra premium, is based on your income from two years ago. So if you are single in 2021 and your income from 2019 exceeded $88,000 or you are married and your combined income exceeded $176,000, you will have to pay increased premiums. The first bracket increase is an extra 40 percent in premiums per person per month.

The higher your income, the more you get to pay. You pay the top premiums once your individual income is over $500,000 or $750,000 for couples. This bracket is a 240 percent increase from the base premium per person per month!

This table shows the Medicare premium brackets for 2021. The Resources page at Divorce-The-IRS.com directs you to more information.

2021

If your filing status and yearly income in 2019 (for what you pay in 2021) was			
File individual tax return	File joint tax return	File married & separate tax return	You pay each month (in 2021)
$88,000 or less	$176,000 or less	$88,000 or less	$148.50
above $88,000 up to $111,000	above $176,000 up to $222,000	Not applicable	$207.90
above $111,000 up to $138,000	above $222,000 up to $276,000	Not applicable	$297.00
above $138,000 up to $165,000	above $276,000 up to $330,000	Not applicable	$386.10
above $165,000 and less than $500,000	above $330,000 and less than $750,000	above $88,000 and less than $412,000	$475.20
$500,000 or above	$750,000 and above	$412,000 and above	$504.90

DEFUSE THIS BOMB BY AVOIDING PROVISIONAL INCOME

What's the secret to avoiding this escalating tax? Well, you can be poor, or utilize tax-free strategies early in your retirement planning that don't produce provisional income. Tax-free withdrawals do not count toward these thresholds, and you can withdraw as much money as you'd like from your tax-free bucket without worrying about taxes on the withdrawals, your Social Security, and now, the extra taxes on your Medicare premiums.

Medicare Part D (which covers prescription drug insurance) also works with income brackets. Here is the 2021 chart for the income brackets and extra tax you get to pay for this benefit in retirement. Again, you can find more details in the Resources section of Divorce-The-IRS.com.

2021

If your filing status and yearly income in 2019 was			
File individual tax return	File joint tax return	File married & separate tax return	You pay each month (in 2021)
$88,000 or less	$176,000 or less	$88,000 or less	your plan premium
above $88,000 up to $111,000	above $176,000 up to $222,000	not applicable	$12.30 + your plan premium
above $111,000 up to $138,000	above $222,000 up to $276,000	not applicable	$31.80 + your plan premium
above $138,000 up to $165,000	above $276,000 up to $330,000	not applicable	$51.20 + your plan premium
above $165,000 and less than $500,000	above $330,000 and less than $750,000	above $88,000 and less than $412,000	$70.70 + your plan premium
$500,000 or above	$750,000 and above	$412,000 and above	$77.10 + your plan premium

If you don't want to pay these extra premiums in retirement and would rather use your money for something a little more fun, start planning now to avoid producing too much provisional income in retirement. This will help you divorce the IRS and keep more money for yourself. And you may need some of that money for your required minimum distributions.

Chapter 11

TAX TIME BOMB 6

REQUIRED MINIMUM DISTRIBUTIONS

By this point, you know that if you take money from your IRA or traditional 401(k), you will owe taxes on it. Now, let's imagine you are lucky to have enough retirement income from other sources, and you haven't touched your tax-deferred accounts yet. Wouldn't it be nice if you could leave those accounts alone to continue their growth, tax-deferred?

It would, but you can't.

The IRS had a lien on those accounts from the moment you contributed your first dollar to them, and you accepted the tax deduction loan they gave you. Like all loans, there comes a time when they are due and you need to start paying. If you haven't started paying on these accounts by the time you are seventy-two years old, the IRS will require it. They tax you through Required Minimum Distributions (RMDs). You can find more details on these in the Resources section of Divorce-The-IRS.com, but we will cover what you need to know here.

HOW REQUIRED MINIMUM DISTRIBUTIONS WORK

Once you turn seventy-two (it used to be age 70.5), you are required to withdraw a certain percentage of all your tax-deferred money based on your age and pay taxes on it. Whether you need the money or not is irrelevant. You have to withdraw it and pay tax.

Starting in 2022, the amount you have to take out at age seventy-two is equal to 3.65 percent of your tax-deferred balances on December 31 of the previous year. The percentage you have to withdraw then increases every year. By the time you are eighty, this percentage will have increased to 4.96 percent. And by ninety, it's 8.20 percent.

This table shows the IRS's new required minimum distribution period based on your age (starting in 2022). As your age goes up, the distribution period goes down. A link to the full table is in the Resources section of Divorce-The-IRS.com.

IRA REQUIRED MINIMUM DISTRIBUTION

Age	Distribution Period (in years)	RMD as % of Account Balance	Age	Distribution Period (in years)	RMD as % of Account Balance
72	27.4	3.65%	97	7.8	12.83%
73	26.5	3.78%	98	7.3	13.70%
74	25.5	3.93%	99	6.8	14.71%
75	24.6	4.07%	100	6.4	15.63%
76	23.7	4.22%	101	6	16.67%
77	22.9	4.37%	102	5.6	17.86%
78	22	4.55%	103	5.2	19.24%
79	21.1	4.74%	104	4.9	20.41%
80	20.2	4.96%	105	4.6	21.74%
81	19.4	5.16%	106	4.3	23.26%
82	18.5	5.41%	107	4.1	24.40%
83	17.7	5.65%	108	3.9	25.65%
84	16.8	5.96%	109	3.7	27.03%
85	16	6.25%	110	3.5	28.58%
86	15.2	6.58%	111	3.4	29.42%
87	14.4	6.95%	112	3.3	30.31%
88	13.7	7.30%	113	3.1	32.26%
89	12.9	7.76%	114	3	33.34%
90	12.2	8.20%	115	2.9	34.49%
91	11.5	8.70%	116	2.8	35.72%
92	10.8	9.26%	117	2.7	37.04%
93	10.1	9.91%	118	2.5	40.00%
94	9.5	10.53%	119	2.3	43.48%
95	8.9	11.24%	120+	2	50.00%
96	8.4	11.91%			

*This is the new RMD table starting in 2022.

A REQUIRED MINIMUM DISTRIBUTION EXAMPLE

Joe Retiree, who is eighty and has an IRA worth $100,000 at the end of last year, would use the Uniform Lifetime Table. The IRS uses several tables to calculate distributions based on personal circumstances. The most common one—

which applies to Joe Retiree and also (probably) you—is the Uniform Lifetime Table.

To calculate the year's minimum distribution amount, we take Joe Retiree's age on December 31 of this year and find the corresponding distribution period in the table. Then, we divide the value of the IRA on December 31 of the previous year by the distribution period to find Joe's required minimum distribution.

This indicates a distribution period of 20.2 years for an eighty-year-old. Therefore, Joe must take out at least $4,950.50 this year ($100,000 divided by 20.2) from his IRA and pay tax on it.

This is why those tax deductions taken during all those years you were working were actually like loans from the IRS. You *have* to pay them back! Even if you don't want to, you have no choice and are mandated by law. If you choose to (or accidentally) break this law, the penalties are stiff. As a penalty, you will owe 50 percent of what you were supposed to withdraw, and then you still have to take out the RMD amount and pay tax on that as well!

DEFUSE THIS BOMB BY UTILIZING TAX-FREE STRATEGIES

There is actually a way to get around RMDs and not be forced to take money out of your accounts and pay taxes.

You guessed it: it's by utilizing tax-free strategies and accounts like the Roth IRA and Roth 401(k). If you are not yet convinced that you should consider paying your taxes now at known, historically low rates and saving your money in tax-free accounts, you could get rocked hard by the next tax explosion, which happens when you outlive your spouse.

Chapter 12

TAX TIME BOMB 7

OUTLIVING YOUR SPOUSE

For most married couples, there is a ticking tax time bomb waiting for them in their golden years. This is a problem that most people don't like to talk about, and is often overlooked until it's too late to do anything about it. But this issue should be discussed as part of any comprehensive financial plan, as there are ways you may be able to defuse the problem if you act early.

This tax time bomb explodes when the first spouse passes away, leaving the surviving spouse to file taxes as a single person.

Often, income doesn't decline much when the first spouse passes. It usually only decreases due to the loss of the smaller Social Security check, as all the income-producing assets owned by the couple transfer to the surviving spouse. But other things do change. The standard tax deduction is cut in half for the surviving spouse, and tax brackets jump considerably for single filers.

Paying a lot of extra tax to the IRS and having a lower standard of living once their spouse has passed isn't what most people are longing for. This tragedy is often referred to as "the widow's penalty."

HOW THE WIDOW'S PENALTY WORKS

Let's look at a married couple, Jim and Sue, and their income.

> $30,000 for Jim's Social Security
> + $20,000 for Sue's Social Security
> + $50,000 in withdrawals from IRAs
> = $100,000 total gross income.

While married and both living, Jim and Sue owe taxes on 85 percent of their Social Security and are able to apply their married filing joint standard deduction against their IRA withdrawals.

> $42,500 as the taxable portion of Social Security
> + $24,900 as the taxable portion of the IRA withdrawal after

standard deduction (which is $25,100 for a married couple over 65 years old)

= $67,400 of total taxable income.

Jim and Sue are in the 12 percent marginal tax bracket and pay an 8.42 percent effective tax rate. They owe $7,784 in federal tax. Their take-home, spendable income is $92,216 a year.

Now if Jim were to pass away, let's see what happens to the income.

$30,000 is Sue's new Social Security amount, as she would get the larger benefit now.

+ $50,000 in withdrawals from IRAs

= $80,000 of total gross income.

Despite now being widowed, 85 percent of Sue's Social Security is still taxable, so her taxable income would look like this:

$25,500 as the taxable portion of Social Security (85 percent of the benefit)

+ $37,450 as the taxable portion of the IRA withdrawal after standard deduction (for a single person)

= $62,950 of total taxable income.

Sue, by herself now, would be in the 22 percent marginal

tax bracket and pay an effective rate of 12.96 percent. She would owe $9,785 in federal tax, which is $2,001 *more* than when she was married, and her take-home income would become $70,215.

Even though her income is considerably less (due to a loss of $20,000 per year from the lost Social Security), Sue pays more tax than when she was married. She jumps in the marginal bracket by 10 percent, and her effective rate jumps by 4.54 percent. This certainly isn't the news Sue wants or needs to hear the year after her husband passes away.

DEFUSE THIS BOMB WITH TWO APPROACHES

Had Jim and Sue planned for a tax-free retirement, they would be withdrawing $50,000 each year from a Roth IRA instead of a traditional IRA. This one change would have moved them from paying taxes in retirement to a 0 percent tax bracket without any taxes in retirement. Their take-home income, together, would have been the full $100,000 per year, and once Jim passed, Sue would have still received all the income ($80,000 now) with $0 in taxes owed to the IRS.

Now, imagine if tax rates increased from here, as is likely. That would make this painful situation even more difficult for Sue, which is sad.

If you are married, this could be a ticking tax time bomb

waiting for you in retirement! It should be discussed and specifically planned for. If you haven't addressed this issue within your retirement plan, please do so as soon as possible. This is another tax time bomb that can be defused by utilizing tax-free bucket accounts.

Withdrawing your income from a Roth or other tax-free account has no impact on your taxes and won't allow the new, single tax bracket or lost tax deduction to affect you once your spouse passes. You can even take more money out of the Roth IRA to make up for the lost Social Security income without having it affecting your tax bill!

The Roth IRA is not the only approach that can be used to defuse some of these tax time bombs. Another approach is the use of life insurance. Some couples purchase a permanent life insurance policy that will pay out when the first spouse passes. The proceeds from life insurance are received by the surviving spouse tax-free and can be used to offset the widow's penalty simply by providing more money to pay the increased tax bills.

Calculating the correct amount of life insurance to purchase for this strategy can be tricky. This is because it depends on factors that are unknowable, like at what age each person will pass. But reasonable assumptions can be made, and with the help of some planning software and a good financial planner, it's possible to figure out the prudent amount of insurance needed to defuse this tax problem.

Although it may be uncomfortable for married couples to discuss what happens after one of them passes, the widow's penalty means it's important to plan for this tax time bomb. With two approaches available—Roth IRAs and life insurance policies—it's possible to defuse this problem, even with the unknowns involved. Unfortunately, though, as we will discover next, it's not just the surviving spouse who pays tax.

Chapter 13

TAX TIME BOMB 8

PAYING TAXES FROM THE GRAVE

Many people would like to leave a legacy to a charity or the ones they love the most. Even if your goal is to "die broke," it's likely you will leave something at the end of your life.

This can be yet another tax time bomb explosion. It's one that *you* light the fuse on, but it doesn't go off until the moment you pass away, leaving a tax burden for the ones you love.

If you've managed your golden years correctly, you have already defused many tax time bombs. Now, you may also have a growing estate and are thinking about passing that money to the next generation. Proper estate planning is designed to avoid you having to pay more to the government than necessary, and to make sure you are passing on as much as possible to your loved ones.

At the end of your life, if you have money in a tax-deferred retirement plan like an IRA or 401(k), you can bequeath it to anyone you choose. But you should know they will have to pay taxes on every penny they inherit from these types of accounts. This can create quite a tax explosion, depending on who inherits your money.

HOW INHERITANCE TAX WORKS

If your spouse inherits your IRA, the process is fairly easy, and they can just combine that money into their own IRA. They still have to pay taxes on the money as they withdraw it, though, at the single tax rate (as we learned with Tax Time Bomb 7). If you pass the money to someone other than your spouse, another explosion starts.

The passage of the new SECURE (Setting Every Community Up for Retirement Enhancement) Act changed the rules for taking money from inherited IRAs. In general, a nonspouse beneficiary will have up to ten years to take out *all* the money from your IRA, and they will pay taxes on every penny!

This can be a bigger explosion than you realize, as the tax rate on that money is now at the beneficiary's rate, and they may still be in their working years, making good money.

Let's say your beneficiaries are your kids. Now that the money is theirs, the withdrawals may be taxed at a higher tax bracket than you were in, or even worse, the money may push your kids into an even higher tax bracket.

DEFUSE THIS BOMB WITH THE SAME STRATEGIES—OR NOT

Some of the people I work with don't care about the tax burden they may leave to their heirs once they have departed this earth. That is okay. I get it. They say their kids should be happy to get anything, and if they have to pay a lot of taxes on the money, so be it. If this is how you feel, there is no need to worry about this tax time bomb.

Others care deeply about this issue. Some people want their loved ones (or chosen charities) to receive every penny they possibly can. Others have a huge dislike for the IRS and don't want to offer them a single penny if they don't have to, If either of these describes you, don't worry. There are ways to defuse this tax bomb.

The two most popular strategies are the same ones used to defuse the last tax time bomb of outliving your spouse. If you planned early, shifted your money to the tax-free bucket, and utilized Roth strategies, you can sleep well knowing that anyone can inherit your Roth accounts completely tax-free. Even if they take every penny out the day they inherit the money, it doesn't matter. It's all tax-free.

The other popular strategy is to make sure you have a permanent life insurance policy in place. Then, when you and your spouse have passed, your heirs will receive enough tax-free life insurance proceeds to cover any taxes due on the other money they inherit from you. There is even a special kind of life insurance designed specifically for this tax time bomb, called second-to-die life insurance.

Second-to-die life insurance is exactly as it sounds. It is a policy based on two people's lives, and it pays out when the second (last) person (spouse) passes away. The kids will then inherit the tax-deferred accounts, and they'll need the life insurance money to pay the tax bills they also inherit. These policies are usually for married couples who want to defuse this last tax time bomb and not pay taxes from their grave. It is best to work with a financial planner or estate attorney if you are considering this strategy, as you care deeply about this issue and you want to get it right.

Now we've discussed all eight tax time bombs that can cause you to pay more than necessary to the IRS. They are exploding tax rates, early withdrawal penalties, sharing your retirement with the IRS, Social Security tax, Medicare premiums, required minimum distributions, outliving your spouse, and paying taxes from the grave. It can feel overwhelming to see all these potential bombs ready to explode, but as I have explained, there are ways to defuse all these bombs.

In Part 3, we will cover what to do with all this information, including how to identify your ideal number, and how to work with Roth strategies and life insurance. Then, we will review some case studies so you can see how these strategies work in the real world. I'll also share some advice for Americans living overseas and for foreign nationals working in America before we bring all of this information together.

Part III

WHAT TO DO
ABOUT IT ALL

Chapter 14

YOUR IDEAL NUMBER

I am sure you have figured out by now that the Roth IRA and Roth 401(k) are two of the main tools you can use to defuse every tax time bomb and officially divorce yourself from the IRS. As you now understand, the benefits of Roth accounts are so much greater than just the tax-free growth most people associate with them. If utilized correctly, they can boost the amount you save for retirement and significantly lower your retirement tax rates, possibly all the way down to 0 percent. They also help you avoid Social Security taxes and Medicare premium hikes. The Roth account even helps you avoid paying tax from the grave! When done well, a person can pay no taxes in retirement. To achieve this, it means using Roth accounts correctly and *in combination with tax-deferred accounts,* as we will discuss in the final part of this book.

We will cover how to calculate your ideal number, how to work with Roth strategies, and discuss considerations for life insurance policies. Then we will examine three case studies of people at various stages in their journey to retirement so you can see what these strategies could look like for you. We will discuss the complications for Americans overseas and foreign nationals working in the US. Then, we will finish by bringing these ideas together so you can take action and set yourself on a path to divorce the IRS. Let's start by looking at the benefits of combining Roth accounts with tax-deferred accounts.

> As awesome as Roth accounts are, the key to building maximum wealth and paying minimal tax, both over your working life and in retirement, is actually a combination strategy which utilizes both tax-deferred and tax-free retirement accounts.

With both types of accounts available, you have the ability to proportionately withdraw money from the account that is most beneficial to you each tax year. This allows you to maximize your standard deduction using tax-deferred money, as well as your tax-free accounts. This is an important concept to understand and a valuable way to boost your wealth. It allows you to turn the tables on the IRS by using their rules to beat them at their own game.

In order to do this correctly, you need to figure out your

ideal number. Under our progressive-style tax system, the first dollars you earn each year are actually tax-free. You receive this income tax-free by utilizing your standard (or itemized) deduction. In 2021, this is $12,550 for individuals and $25,100 for married couples filing jointly. If you are older than sixty-five or blind, your standard deduction is even greater, with an extra $1,700 for single taxpayers and $2,700 for those who are married. This is the amount of income you can "write off" and not pay taxes on each year. The amount increases over time, as it is indexed to inflation.

UTILIZING STANDARD DEDUCTIONS

John is retired and would like to withdraw $100,000 a year from his retirement accounts. He has no other income. When John files his taxes, he is allowed to apply his standard deduction. He gets to "write off" the first $12,550 (the 2021 standard deduction) of his income as tax-free. This leaves John with only $87,450 of withdrawals that could be subject to tax, using the progressive brackets we discussed at the beginning of this book.

If John is entitled to the first $12,550 of his income tax-free, why not take that retirement income from a source he would normally have to pay taxes on? It makes perfect sense to withdraw his first $12,550 from a tax-deferred account like an IRA and then use the standard deduction to offset the tax owed on this money. This is money John has never been taxed on because it was saved earlier in life, in a pre-tax account. And now, done correctly, he can withdraw and spend this money, all without ever paying any taxes on it!

If John withdraws more than the standard deduction from a tax-deferred account—say, $12,600 from his IRA—he would now owe taxes at the lowest tax bracket of 10 percent, but only on the $50 that exceeds his standard deduction.

> This means you can receive a tax deduction when you contribute money to an IRA or traditional 401(k) and not pay any taxes when you withdraw. This tax deduction isn't a loan; it is a true wealth-building opportunity for you to legally cheat the IRS out of a little tax money!

Although I've highlighted Roth accounts throughout this book, I am also saying you need some money in tax-deferred accounts as well. You just don't need that much, and probably less than you already have in these types of accounts. So what is the ideal number, and how do you figure that out?

CALCULATING YOUR IDEAL NUMBER FOR TAX-DEFERRED ACCOUNTS

Most people I sit down with to discuss taxes and financial planning already have significant sums in tax-deferred accounts—more than needed to maximize this bucket for lifetime tax planning. For most people, it's time to stop contributing to the "tax me later" bucket (taking IRS loans) and start building the "tax me never" bucket as much as possible.

How much you need in tax-deferred accounts when you reach retirement depends on many factors and should be calculated within your unique financial plan. It will depend on the future amount of your Social Security benefit and when you choose to claim it, as well as other factors like the amount of money you have invested in taxable accounts and whether or not you will receive a pension. But as a general rule:

> By the time you are seventy-two and subject to RMDs, your balances in tax-deferred accounts should be low enough that your RMD is equal to or less than your standard deduction.

To determine if your balances in tax-deferred accounts are already too big, you have to calculate how long you have until retirement, how much you are contributing, and the expected growth on these assets. I have built a calculator you can use to find your ideal number at Divorce-The-IRS.com. If you have more than your ideal number in this bucket, consider using the shifting and conversion strategies discussed in the next chapter.

This discussion shows the enormous benefits of Roth

accounts when utilized correctly. However, this means using them in combination with tax-deferred accounts, utilizing standard deductions, and calculating your ideal number. This is so when you are seventy-two, your balances in tax-deferred accounts are low enough to avoid unnecessary taxes forced upon you by RMDs. It is a great strategy, and as we are about to discuss, there may be even more Roth strategies available to you.

Chapter 15

ROTH STRATEGIES

Once you know your ideal number and have a plan to arrive at that number at the correct age, it's time to figure out how to get the rest of your money into the tax-free bucket.

The tax-free accounts that will be utilized most heavily by the most people are the Roth IRA and Roth 401(k). Some people may also utilize cash-value life insurance as a tax-free tool, which we will discuss more about in the next chapter. For now, let's learn a little more about Roth accounts and some unique strategies you can use to shift or divert more of your assets and income into these tools.

THE ROTH IRA

Roth IRAs have been around since 1997 and were named after William Roth, a former Delaware senator. They are straightforward accounts that anyone can get money into, one way or another. Here are some of the basic rules you should know about Roth IRAs:

1. They can only be contributed to with earned income, so if you don't have a job, you can't contribute directly into a Roth IRA.
2. They need to be open for at least five years before the growth or interest can be withdrawn tax-free (even if you are over 59.5 years old).
3. The amount you can contribute directly will change periodically. In 2021, the contribution limit is $6,000 a year unless you are over fifty, in which case you can deposit up to $7,000.
4. Almost all brokerage firms, both physical and online, offer Roth IRAs. Most banks and investment companies do, also.
5. You can't contribute to a Roth IRA directly if you make too much money. In 2021, the limit for singles was $140,000. For married couples, the limit was $208,000. There is a phase-out as you approach these limits. However, there are legal ways around this rule, and we'll discuss these later in this book.

Here is a table showing the income limits and phase-outs for contributing directly to a Roth (or traditional) IRA:

2021

Filing Status	Modified adjusted gross income (MAGI)	Contribution Limit
Single individuals	< $125,000	$6,000
	≥ $125,000 but < $140,000	Partial contribution
	≥ $140,000	Not eligible
Married (filing joint returns)	< $198,000	$6,000
	≥ $198,000 but < $208,000	Partial contribution
	≥ $208,000	Not eligible
Married (filing separately)*	Not eligible	$6,000
	< $10,000	Partial contribution
	≥ $10,000	Not eligible

*Married (filing separately) can use the limits for single individuals if they have not lived with their spouse in the past year.

Working with people on their financial plans, I find the most important of all these rules is number two listed in the table: the five-year rule. You need to have your Roth IRA open for at least five years to take any growth from the Roth tax-free (known as a qualified distribution). This clock starts on January 1 of the year you make your first contribution to a Roth IRA. Any Roth opened at any time in your life starts this important clock. If you have never had a Roth IRA, you should consider opening one just to start this clock. Even if you only contribute $1 to your new Roth, it counts. Once the five years have been satisfied, you never have to worry about this rule again.

TWO LITTLE-KNOWN WAYS TO FUND A ROTH IRA (EVEN IF YOU MAKE TOO MUCH MONEY)

Many people don't think they can contribute to a Roth IRA because they earn more than the allowable income limits (refer to the table in the last section). And while they may not be able to contribute directly, there are several other ways to get money into a Roth IRA, and anyone can use these strategies. Here are two you may not know about.

BACKDOOR ROTH IRA STRATEGY

The first strategy is the backdoor Roth IRA strategy, and it has been around for many years. It's a completely legal way for high earners to fund Roth IRAs, and the strategy is straightforward. You contribute the allowable, nondeductible traditional IRA amount for the year, which is $6,000 for people under fifty and $7,000 for people fifty and older in 2021. Then later, you convert that money to a Roth IRA. This works because there are no income limits for contributing to a nondeductible IRA, and there are also no income limits for converting an IRA to a Roth IRA.

Just fill out IRS form 8606 and submit it with your taxes in the year you do this to show that your IRA contribution was nondeductible (not pre-tax). The strategy gets a little trickier if you have other IRAs or rollovers out there, so contact a financial advisor or your tax professional to make sure this is the right strategy for you before executing. You can also learn more about this strategy by visiting the Resources page at Divorce-The-IRS.com

MEGA-BACKDOOR ROTH STRATEGY

This strategy utilizes your 401(k) at work, where you may already have a 401(k) Roth option. If you do, that's great, and yet another way to fund a Roth without income restrictions. If you have a regular 401(k) without a Roth option, you can probably still use it to ultimately fund a Roth IRA for yourself.

Have you ever noticed when you make your 401(k) elections that you can specify if you would like to make after-tax contributions? Almost all plans have this option, but almost no one chooses it. If you put money into this option, it comes out of your paycheck after it has been taxed, just like a Roth, and is invested tax-deferred into your 401(k).

This works like a Roth because when you leave your job one day and roll over that 401(k), all the money you contributed after tax is eligible to roll directly into a Roth IRA. Some plans even allow in-service withdrawals of after-tax monies, meaning you can move it into your Roth even while you are still employed and contributing. Check with your plan administrator to learn about the specific rules for your plan.

This strategy also allows you to put in more than the direct annual contribution limits, since the total annual limit for contributing (from all sources) to your 401(k) in 2021 is $58,000 for people under fifty and $64,500 for those fifty and over.

Deciding if either of these strategies is right for you involves a fair amount of financial planning and tax projections. If you would like help figuring out if you should use either strategy to fund a Roth IRA, do your research or contact a fiduciary financial planner for help.

ROTH CONVERSIONS

The Roth conversion provides another underutilized opportunity. This is a simple way to shift dollars from the "tax me later" bucket to the "tax me never" bucket. It is done by simply moving (converting) some or all of the money in a tax-deferred account into a Roth account. This creates a tax liability that year on all the dollars you shift, so the strategy must be considered carefully. However, once converted, the money (and its growth) should never be taxed again.

With the historically low tax rates we are experiencing, it's worth determining if this strategy is right for you. This is akin to locking in the current (historically low) tax rates now and then never having to worry about it again. As a financial advisor, I find it surprising that people are so reluctant to lock in the current, historically low tax rate and move forward tax-free, especially when they are so keen to do this with mortgages, which are basically the same idea, and they are happy to pay lots of fees to lock in the rate.

Luckily, you can convert just the amounts you'd like into a Roth IRA. This allows you to strategically plan with precision what's best for you to shift between buckets and pay tax on each year. You likely don't want to push yourself into a higher marginal tax bracket with your conversion, but maximizing your current bracket can make a lot of sense.

If you choose to convert to a Roth IRA and are younger than 59.5, make sure you have money available to pay the tax bill. Allowing the account to pay the tax bill for you will result in the 10 percent early withdrawal penalty being levied on the amount withdrawn. This penalty (Tax Time Bomb 2) negates the benefits of the conversion in most cases.

It's also important to understand the government has imposed the five-year rule on Roth conversions to prevent people from converting an IRA to a Roth and then immediately withdrawing their money, thus sidestepping the 10 percent early withdrawal penalty. This rule simply states that any money converted to a Roth IRA needs to stay in that Roth account for five years to qualify for penalty-free distribution. This time period begins January 1 of the year you convert. However, if you are over 59.5 years old, this rule does not affect you.

THE 72(T) AND 72(Q)

The 72(t) and 72(q) strategies are known by those who are seriously investigating the idea of retiring before they are 59.5 years old. These numbers reference the portion of the IRS code that allows a person to access money in the "tax me later" bucket, like from their IRA or 401(k), before they are 59.5 years old without incurring the 10 percent early withdrawal penalty. The 72(t) applies to IRAs and other qualified monies and the 72(q) to non-qualified money like non-qualified annuities (which are tax-deferred investments).

If you are serious about divorcing the IRS and living a tax-free retirement, it is vitally important to understand these legal strategies because the biggest impediment to Roth conversions is the whopping tax bill that comes with converting. Paying tax on all that tax-deferred money is a hard pill to swallow, even if you know you will owe all that tax (and likely more) down the road anyway. This tax bill stops most people from converting their money. Coupled with the fact that if you are under 59.5 years old, you can't use any of the money from the conversion account to pay the tax as to avoid the 10 percent early withdrawal penalty, conversions feel out of reach for many people. They don't have to be, though, with proper planning.

The 72(t) and 72(q) allow you to carve off a portion of your tax-deferred bucket money and start withdrawing it at any age, without any 10 percent early withdrawal penalty. You will still owe tax on the money taken out, but you were going to owe those taxes anyway, whether you took the money out now or later. This creates a stream of income each year. You can use the money to pay for the taxes caused by enacting Roth conversions on another portion of your tax-deferred money. This allows you to use the money in your tax-deferred bucket to pay the taxes due on the conversions without subjecting yourself to the 10 percent early withdrawal penalty.

Of course, there are several rules surrounding 72(t) and 72(q) that you should know about. It is best for most people interested in this strategy to work with a qualified financial advisor to make sure they are following all the rules and that it makes good sense within the context of their overall financial plan.

Here are the most important rules you need to know about this strategy:

- If you start this strategy, you must keep it going for five years or until you are 59.5 years old, whichever period is longer. You can stop the program once this requirement has been met, if you'd like.
- You cannot take out any amount of money you choose. There are three approved IRS methods for calculating how much you can withdraw each year, all resulting in

different amounts of money. They are the Required Minimum Distribution (RMD) method, the annuitization method, and the amortization method.

- The annuitization and amortization methods allow you to withdraw greater amounts of money but require you to withdraw the same amount each year. The RMD method allows smaller withdrawals but lets you to calculate the amount each year based on a life expectancy table. This will result in a different amount you can withdraw each year.
- If you choose the annuitization or amortization method for your calculation, you can switch (one time only) to the RMD method. However, you cannot switch the other way, from RMD to either of the other two methods.

Another very beneficial provision is that you can apply this strategy to just a portion of your tax-deferred money. This is usually accomplished by moving only what you would like to run your 72(t) and 72(q) calculations on into a separate IRA. Then you have control over this strategy and can be precise in how you withdraw money for the tax bills created by your conversion.

If you are a little closer to the retirement finish line than the starting line and want a more in-depth look at using 72(t) and 72(q), read the second case study coming up in this book. I outline exactly how my example couple utilizes this strategy to get large amounts of money converted to tax-free accounts and how it all works out for them.

"Measure twice and cut once" is a great saying. Make sure to employ this wisdom when executing Roth conversion strategies. It used to be that if you made a mistake or didn't have the money to pay the IRS tax bill, you could simply change your mind on the deal and recharacterize the money back to your IRA, basically undoing what you did and reversing the tax bill. This is no longer a possibility under the new tax laws, and once the money has been converted, there is no going back. It's permanent.

With careful planning, though, you don't need to make mistakes in executing Roth strategies. Whatever your current situation, there are many options, from regular funding of a Roth IRA to the backdoor strategy, the mega-backdoor strategy, conversions, and the 72(t) and 72(q). They are all worth considering before you look at life insurance, which we will discuss next.

Chapter 16

LIFE INSURANCE FOR TAX-FREE RETIREMENT PLANNING

Life insurance retirement plans (LIRPs) have been around for some time and seem to come and go in popularity. Their popularity appears to be directly correlated with how many life insurance salespeople are out there selling them.

I am torn on the effectiveness of LIRPs. I have seen some work well, and I have seen many of them fail, costing people a lot of their hard-earned money. They are worth mentioning, though, so I am going to point out the benefits, pitfalls, and who should and should not consider them.

There have been a lot of flavors of LIRPs over the years.

They started out with the old, whole life policies which are still around. However, people were not happy with the low savings rate types of returns, so the next version to emerge was universal life. This allowed you to invest into the insurance company's investment portfolio and usually earn a higher rate of return than what whole life policies offered. Next came variable universal life (VUL). People wanted to control their own investing and choose investments tied to the stock and bond markets. The VUL allowed people to choose from a myriad of mutual fund portfolios (called sub-accounts) within their life insurance policies. The insured bore all the investment risk in these policies.

The latest flavor of LIRP uses indexed universal life (IUL) policies. With these, you split the investment risk with the insurance company, usually by investing into a stock index with a limit on the amount you can earn over a stated time period. In return, there is no chance of a negative return if the index goes south. These IUL policies draw on the strength of all the previous versions of permanent cash value policies and are generally the most suitable type of policy to use for a LIRP.

The key difference between all these policies and regular, term life insurance is that they have an investment component. The general goal of term life insurance is to purchase the most amount of death benefit for the least amount of money. The opposite is true for a cash value policy used for LIRP purposes. You want to put in the absolute most amount of money and buy the least amount of insurance allowed by law. This will allow the policy to remain tax-free for you.

FACTORS TO CONSIDER

The first thing worth mentioning about LIRPs is that you need to qualify for the life insurance component. To get any cash value life insurance policy, you have to go through something called underwriting. This is where the life insurance company asks you to complete a physical, usually taking blood and urine to determine your overall health and determine whether or not you qualify for the life insurance. This is the first hurdle that must be crossed for you to even consider a LIRP.

Second, you should really have a need to purchase life insurance, as well as a plan for retirement. This is a life insurance policy, after all, and you will be paying money every month from the investments in the policy to the insurance company for the insurance coverage. This amount can be substantial and depends on both your age and level of health. There are often other costs associated with these types of life insurance policies you will need to consider, such as administration and investment load charges.

So, assuming you need life insurance and you qualify for

it at a rate you are happy to pay, there are a couple of other factors to consider. Many life insurance salespeople would adamantly disagree, but I believe LIRPs should be the last place used to stash money in the tax-free bucket for retirement planning. LIRPs are generally only for those who have:

- Maxed out their Roth 401(k).
- Maxed out a personal Roth (usually via the backdoor strategy).
- Maxed out after-tax contributions they can make to their workplace plan (via the mega-backdoor Roth strategy).
- Completed all the Roth conversions available to them.
- Maxed out any self-employment retirement plan they can contribute to.
- Maxed out their ideal number for the tax-deferred bucket.
- Accumulated too much retirement money in the non-qualified "tax me now" bucket.

As you can imagine, these requirements generally knock most people out of the running for considering a LIRP. But for those who meet all the requirements and still have significant sums of money available to save, a LIRP can be a good option when done correctly.

FULLY FUNDING LIRPS

If you are going to consider a LIRP, please make sure you have the money to fund it to the maximum for the amount of insurance you are purchasing. These plans work best when they are fully funded, and you can put as much money into them as allowed by the law. This gives the plan the best chance for compounded growth and to overcome all the costs associated with the policies.

I have seen too many people get talked into purchasing a LIRP policy—they're told they can just put a little bit of money in and save more over time. This information usually comes from a salesperson who can only sell—you guessed it—life insurance. If the only tool you have or can sell is a hammer, everything out there looks like a nail. Please consider this analogy when listening to a life insurance (hammer only) salesperson. It is best to purchase a LIRP from a tax-free fiduciary planning specialist (not a life insurance salesperson), and only if you meet all the criteria previously mentioned. A fiduciary planner can usually shop around all the life insurance companies and will know where the best deals can be found on LIRP policies.

When you only put a small amount of money into a LIRP, the ongoing costs for insurance and other charges usually eat up all the growth potential of the policy. You continue to feed the policy with your hard-earned money, and in turn, the policy feeds the hungry fees of the insurance company.

In the end, the life insurance company has all the money you contributed, the insurance salesperson makes a big commission, and you don't have much of anything.

If you do have the money to properly purchase and fund a LIRP, great. So why does this work well as a tax-free investment, and how do you use it for tax-free income in retirement?

LIRP COMPLICATIONS

The government likes encouraging people to purchase life insurance. It is better for the government to have a widow or widower receive a big, tax-free life insurance check when a breadwinner passes, rather than being forced into welfare programs. So to encourage life insurance, the federal government allows, within limits, the cash value investments inside life insurance policies to grow tax-deferred. You are allowed to borrow against these investments tax-free from the insurance company, with the investments as collateral.

It sounds a bit complicated, doesn't it?

It is, and this is a big deterrent to using LIRPs. Managing the moving parts of a LIRP is complicated, and it's best done by a good financial planner who utilizes LIRPs on a regular basis. Done incorrectly, these plans can become tax nightmares, not the tax-free investments you originally planned for them to be.

For example, if you put even $1 too much into a LIRP, it becomes something called a modified endowment contract (MEC) and loses the tax-free status you were planning on. Whoops!

If you borrow too much from a LIRP or stop funding your LIRP and the life insurance policy lapses, everything you ever took out of the policy above your cost basis becomes taxable to you in that year, and the plan blows up. Whoops!

The insurance company also has the right to lower the cap over time on the maximum amount you can earn from the indexes in IUL policies. You cannot control this. It is set by the insurance company. If they do this, and they often do, your earning potential can be severely limited. They can't change the fact that you cannot lose any money in the index, though. This fact is protected and valuable.

You also need to understand you won't participate in any of the payable dividends from the companies in the index you choose. The most popular index used in LIRPs is the S&P 500, which is a market capitalization-weighted price index composed of 500 widely held common stocks. Although this is the stated index, you don't actually invest directly into it, and thus you don't receive any of the dividends from the companies in the index.

Dividends on the S&P 500 are a large component of the

long-term growth of the index, and you will always be missing out on that component within an IUL policy used as a LIRP (or any annuity that uses this investment strategy, as well). Unfortunately, this inconvenient fact is always left out of any sales presentation given on an indexed investment, like life insurance or annuities.

So how big of a deal are the dividends in the S&P 500? Let's have a look.

The Power of Dividends and Compounding
Growth of $10,000 (12/1960–12/2018)

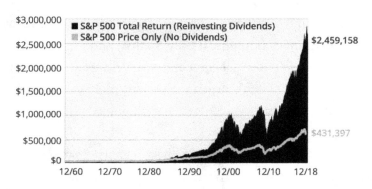

Data Sources: Morningstar and Hartford Funds, 1/19.

The chart shows the S&P 500 Index total return, including reinvesting dividends, compared to a version with no dividends to reinvest. As you can see, dividends play a major role in the long-term growth of an index investment. Within your LIRP indexed investments, you won't be participating in this portion of growth.

These plans all come with long surrender charges, meaning you cannot cancel or get your money out of them without big penalties from the insurance company. Most insurance companies have a ten-year surrender penalty on their policies, and I have even seen some as long as fifteen or twenty years.

My goal isn't to scare you away from a LIRP—at least not entirely, anyway. I just want you to understand some of the risks and who the plan is really designed to help. If you make $1 million a year, a LIRP (and a good planner) is probably right for you.

If I help just one person who shouldn't buy a LIRP avoid buying it, the time it took to write this book will have been worth it to me. I hate to see people purchase bad products that aren't suitable for them and then lose money.

Chapter 17

CASE STUDY 1

DONE RIGHT FROM THE START

In the next three chapters, I'll share three case studies. The first illustrates how a young person starting their career can structure their savings to ultimately end up paying no tax in retirement.

The second demonstrates what a couple closer to retirement should consider. This couple already finds themselves with more than their ideal number in their tax-deferred bucket. They can use the strategies outlined in this book to rectify their situation and arrive at a tax-free retirement.

The final case study discusses how a pension may make it impossible to pay no taxes in retirement, and how to get as close to $0 tax as possible if you will be receiving a taxable pension one day.

Here is a simple example of someone who did it right early in life, was able to achieve a 0 percent tax bracket, and paid no taxes over the course of their retirement.

DOING IT RIGHT FROM THE START

Mary, like many of us, spent most of the money she earned in her twenties. She also had some "life happens" events where she was forced to withdraw the small sums of money she had saved for retirement up to that point. But once Mary turned thirty, she got a little wiser, learned a few things about financial planning by working with a good fiduciary planner who specialized in creating tax-free retirements, and set herself on a solid path to retirement. Here is what she did from ages thirty to sixty.

Mary had a good job that offered both a traditional 401(k) and a Roth 401(k) option. Her company also offered a dollar-for-dollar match on the first 3 percent she contributed to the plan (either traditional or Roth). She decided to put 8 percent of her salary into the Roth 401(k) portion of her plan at work, which made her eligible for the company match. However, the company put their 3 percent match into the traditional 401(k) plan. Mary also opened up a personal Roth IRA and contributed the maximum of $6,000 allowed by law to this account.

To make this easy, let's assume Mary makes $100,000 per year, never gets a raise, and also never increases her retirement contributions. Mary selected some growth-type diversified mutual funds and, over the next thirty years, averaged an 8 percent return each year.

> 8 percent into the Roth 401(k), which is $8,000 each year
>
> + 6 percent of her income into a personal Roth IRA, which is $6,000 each year
>
> = 14 percent of her total income saved for retirement, which is $14,000 per year
>
> + the 3 percent match from her employer into the traditional 401(k), which is $3,000 each year
>
> = a total of $17,000 in savings per year for retirement

This table shows us what happened with that money.

MARY

Age	3% Match (Trad 401k)	8% Roth 401(k) Contribution	Personal Roth IRA
30	$3,000.00	$8,000.00	$6,000.00
31	$6,240.00	$16,640.00	$12,480.00
32	$9,739.20	$25,971.20	$19,478.40
33	$13,518.34	$36,048.90	$27,036.67
34	$17,599.80	$46,932.81	$35,199.61
35	$22,007.79	$58,687.43	$44,015.57
36	$26,768.41	$71,382.43	$53,536.82
37	$31,909.88	$85,093.02	$63,819.77
38	$37,462.67	$99,900.46	$74,925.35
39	$43,459.69	$115,892.50	$86,919.37
40	$49,936.46	$133,163.90	$99,872.92
41	$56,931.38	$151,817.01	$113,862.76
42	$64,485.89	$171,962.37	$128,971.78
43	$72,644.76	$193,719.36	$145,289.52
44	$81,456.34	$217,216.91	$162,912.68
45	$90,972.85	$242,594.26	$181,945.70
46	$101,250.68	$270,001.81	$202,501.35
47	$112,350.73	$299,601.95	$224,701.46
48	$124,338.79	$331,570.11	$248,677.58
49	$137,285.89	$366,095.71	$274,571.79
50	$151,268.76	$403,383.37	$302,537.53
51	$166,370.27	$443,654.04	$332,740.53
52	$182,679.89	$487,146.36	$365,359.77
53	$200,294.28	$534,118.07	$400,588.56
54	$219,317.82	$584,847.52	$438,635.64
55	$239,863.25	$639,635.32	$479,726.49
56	$262,052.31	$698,806.15	$524,104.61
57	$286,016.49	$762,710.64	$572,032.98
58	$311,897.81	$831,727.49	$623,795.62
59	$339,849.63	$906,265.69	$679,699.27
60	$370,037.60	$986,766.94	$740,075.21
Total Value at Age 60	**$2,096,879.76**		

Preparing to retire at age sixty, Mary has over $2 million saved. Most of it is in the tax-free accounts, and she has $370,000 in the tax-deferred bucket from the company match. She rolls over the match portion of her 401(k) to an IRA and combines her Roth 401(k) into her personal

Roth account to simplify her financial life and consolidate the number of accounts she has to manage. Let's see how she structures this in retirement to remain in a 0 percent tax bracket.

AGE SIXTY TO SIXTY-NINE

For the first ten years of retirement, Mary draws $12,550 out of her tax-deferred, traditional IRA account. She withdraws this amount as she is able to apply her standard tax deduction ($12,550 in 2021) against this income and receive it tax-free. She never paid tax on this money as she earned it because it was pre-tax money, and she is now receiving it tax-free in retirement. Nice!

She also takes money out of her Roth account. She uses the 4 percent rule to be conservative, which gives her about $69,000 of income in her first year of retirement. In total, she took $81,550 ($12,550 from her IRA plus $69,000 from her Roth IRA), all tax-free her first year.

She also increases her withdrawal amount by 3 percent each year to keep up with inflation. This is all 100 percent tax-free, and she is in the 0 percent tax bracket for this first decade of retirement. Well done.

At age sixty-five, Mary signed up for Medicare parts A, B and D. But since she wasn't breaching any IRS income thresholds with provisional income for premium rate hikes (Tax Time Bomb 4), she was able to get part A for free. She also got parts B and D for the lowest possible monthly premiums available to her with no surcharges.

AGE SEVENTY TO SEVENTY-ONE

At age seventy, Mary needs to start claiming her Social Security, as waiting beyond seventy to claim it has no benefit. She could have started taking her benefit as early as age sixty-two at a reduced rate, but by waiting until seventy, she has maximized her lifetime benefit and will receive the highest monthly benefit available to her. This comes out to $2,500 a month, or $30,000 a year.

The IRS is will now look at her provisional income to determine if she will owe taxes on her Social Security. The calculation for Mary is fairly simple, as the only provisional income she has is half of her Social Security, which is $15,000 a year, and any amount she withdraws from her traditional IRA.

Mary wants to stay under the $25,000 IRS threshold so she won't owe any taxes on her Social Security. She already uses up $15,000 of the $25,000 threshold with half of her Social Security. So she takes out $10,000 from her traditional IRA account now to get her right up to the $25,000 threshold, but not over.

She doesn't owe any taxes on the $10,000 she took from her tax-deferred traditional IRA because she applies her standard deduction against that money to receive it tax-free.

She doesn't owe any tax on her Social Security because she has remained under the $25,000 threshold with her provisional income.

Because she has been giving herself a 3 percent raise each year to keep up with inflation, she is now withdrawing just over $90,000 from her Roth IRA at age seventy, which doesn't affect her taxes or provisional income.

Mary is now receiving $130,000 ($10,000 from her IRA plus $30,000 from Social Security plus $90,000 from her Roth IRA) in retirement income, all tax-free. She is still in a 0 percent tax bracket. Well done.

AGE SEVENTY-TWO AND BEYOND

Starting at age seventy-two, Mary will be subject to RMDs, as discussed in Tax Time Bomb 6. However, the only money she has that is subject to RMDs is in her tax-deferred account—her old employer match account that she rolled over into her traditional IRA. She has been spending down this account over the past twelve years, applying the standard deductions, and only has $270,000 in this account now. Her RMD at age seventy-two on the amount in this account is $9,854. This is the amount she can withdraw from her IRA to satisfy the RMD, excluding the income from taxes using her standard deduction, and staying under the threshold that would make her Social Security taxable. Mary now has over $135,000 in total retirement income, completely tax-free. Well done, Mary.

RMDs do increase over time, so in the future, Mary may find herself in a situation where her RMD may push her into the lowest tax bracket (which is 10 percent in 2021), and she will have to make a choice: pay a small amount of tax on a couple thousand dollars, or remain tax-free by utilizing a gifting strategy.

If Mary's IRA continues to grow and her RMDs become too great for her to stay in the 0 percent tax bracket, she has the opportunity to gift some of her IRA to charity or maybe to a favorite niece. This would lower the balance of her tax-deferred account to the exact amount that would keep her RMD in the 0 percent tax bracket. She feels better about making a small gift to charity, her niece, or both, rather than giving her money to the IRS.

Over the course of her thirty-year retirement, Mary receives approximately $3,280,000 from her Roth IRA, $500,000 from Social Security, and $300,000 from her tax-deferred account, for a total of more than $4 million. She received every penny of this income completely tax-free.

Mary didn't save anything on her taxes while she was working those thirty years at her job, as she didn't put any of
her own money into a tax-deferred account. Her friends all
used conventional wisdom and saved the same 14 percent
that Mary did over the same thirty years. They all put 8
percent of their salary into the traditional 401(k), received
the 3 percent match, and started personal traditional IRAs
to save $6,000 each year and write off even more of their
taxes. This saved each of Mary's friends about $3,080 a
year in taxes while they were working. Over the thirty-
year period in this example, that adds up to tax savings of
$92,400 for each of Mary's friends.

In retirement, though, Mary's friends not only owed taxes
on everything they took out of their tax-deferred accounts,
but they also made 85 percent of their Social Security taxable. At age seventy-two, Mary was able to take out over
$135,000 in tax-free income, whereas her friends only had
about $110,000 left to spend after they paid the IRS. Over
the course of their thirty-year retirement, each of Mary's
friends paid the IRS almost $1 million in total tax. Would
you like to be Mary or one of Mary's friends? If you are early
in your career, you have the opportunity to choose now.

Chapter 18

CASE STUDY 2

CLOSER TO THE FINISH LINE

I hope that lots of young people will read this book, follow its advice, and easily be able to save as much money as Mary did in our first case study. It is likely, though, that many people reading this book won't be able to apply all the principles from the start of their career. Maybe you are one of those people who is closer to the finish line than the starting line. That's okay, too, and the principles of this book can still be cleverly applied to almost any situation or age. Here is a case study spotlighting a couple in their fifties who are closing in on retirement.

Bob and Helen are both fifty years old and have always been savers, but being busy living their lives, they haven't taken the time to understand taxes or focus on a specific retirement plan. They both have great careers that they love, and each makes $120,000 a year. They have been putting 10 percent of their salaries into their traditional 401(k)s every year since they were both thirty years old and have rolled those accounts over into their IRA each time they changed companies. They would like to be done working and start travelling the world at age sixty-five. Here is what they have now:

$500,000 in each of their IRAs

+ $250,000 in each of their traditional 401(k)s at work

= $1,500,000 in total retirement tax-deferred assets

+ $120,000 in a non-qualified, joint mutual fund account

They are squarely in the 24 percent marginal tax bracket, and the mortgage on their home is set to be paid off at the same time they would like to retire. They meet with a fiduciary financial planner who specializes in tax-free retirement planning to craft a plan. Let's break down what they should do, step by step.

STEP 1: STOP CONTRIBUTIONS TO THE TRADITIONAL 401(K)S

Bob has access to a Roth 401(k) at his workplace, so he starts by switching his 10 percent contribution to the Roth option and away from the traditional 401(k) option. This decreases his take-home pay by the amount he was saving (borrowing from the IRS) in taxes, which is $240 a month, but Bob feels he can absorb that small dip in his monthly pay without a problem. All of his contributions ($12,000 a year) will now be fully owned by him, and there won't be an IRS lien on the money contributed to the Roth 401(k) plan going forward.

Helen's employer does not offer a Roth 401(k) option, but they do allow after-tax contributions into the plan. Helen redirects her 10 percent contribution from the traditional 401(k) option into the after-tax plan option. This also decreases her take-home pay by the amount she was saving in taxes, which was $240 a month, but she also feels she can live with her new take-home pay amount. She understands this is an easy way to boost her retirement savings, as we discussed in Part 1 of this book.

STEP 2: ROTH CONVERSIONS

Both Bob and Helen can start converting their IRAs into Roth IRAs as there are no income limits or restrictions in doing so. They will owe taxes, though, on every dollar they convert. Working with their new tax-free retirement planning specialist, they come up with a plan to start converting $50,000 from each of their IRAs every year into their new Roth IRA accounts, and will pay the tax on this money now. They understand they will have to pay the tax on all this money someday anyway, and they feel comfortable paying it now at their known, 24 percent tax rate. They do not feel tax rates are likely to decrease in the future.

By converting $100,000 ($50,000 each), they remain under the $329,850 threshold that would put them in the 32 percent tax bracket, based on 2021 tax rates. Their income now looks like this:

$214,900 from their combined, taxable salaries after applying their standard deduction

+ $100,000 from the amount they are converting from IRAs to Roth IRAs

+ $10,000 of interest and growth from their mutual fund account

= $324,900 of total taxable income (which is under the $329,850 threshold that defines the 32 percent bracket in 2021)

This conversion will increase their tax burden each year by $24,000, since they are in the 24 percent tax bracket. They plan on paying this extra tax bill from their non-qualified mutual fund account, as we will see in the next step.

STEP 3: REDUCE THE "TAX ME NOW" NON-QUALIFIED TAX BUCKET

Bob and Helen understand they have more than they need in their non-qualified mutual fund account. They both have stable jobs and feel that $50,000 in this account would suffice as an emergency fund and keep them comfortable. This leaves about $75,000 they can shift from this account to help with the overall retirement plan. They direct this money ($24,000 a year) toward paying the tax bill on the Roth conversion strategy from step 2 over a three-year period.

STEP 4: A 72(T) CONVERSION STRATEGY

The money in the non-qualified account was used over the three years to pay the tax bill on the conversions from step 2. But after three years, the money to pay the tax bills ran out.

Over the three years of conversions, Bob and Helen were able to move $300,000 from their IRAs to their new Roth IRAs. Their Roth accounts have also started the five-year rule clock, and they only have two years left until they satisfy this rule and the money can be withdrawn without taxes or penalties.

They still have $700,000 in their IRAs they would like to convert to their Roth accounts. They do not want to use the accounts to pay the taxes, as this would also trigger the 10 percent early withdrawal penalties, since they are still both under 59.5 years old. This would negate the value of this strategy. They decide to use a 72(t) strategy to access their IRA accounts without the 10 percent penalty.

They would like to remain in the 24 percent tax bracket, so they structure the strategy like this:

Bob sets up a 72(t) (substantially equal payments) plan on the remaining $350,000 in his IRA. This allows him to withdraw about $12,500 a year from his IRA without having to pay the 10 percent early withdrawal penalty. He will have to continue this plan and take out the $12,500 each year for at least five years, or until he is 59.5, whichever period is greater. Bob will be required to stay with this plan until he is 59.5, as that is the longer period of time.

The new $12,500 that Bob now has access to each year gives Bob and Helen the ability to continue the Roth conversion strategy on Helen's IRA and to pay the extra tax bill with the money Bob is receiving from the 72(t) plan. This new income will now allow Helen to convert $50,000 each year, and the $12,000 in taxes can be paid for with Bob's 72(t) plan money.

The couple does this until age sixty, when they no longer have to continue the 72(t) plan, and Helen's IRA has been completely converted to her Roth IRA.

Bob still has around $300,000 in his traditional IRA, the one he had been taking the 72(t) money from.

STEP 5: MORE CONVERSIONS

Now that the couple is older than 59.5, Bob can stop the 72(t) payments. He's eligible to access his IRA without any 10 percent early withdrawal penalty. He can now start converting the rest of his traditional IRA to his Roth IRA and use some of the money from the withdrawal to pay the taxes as he goes.

The couple still wants to remain in the 24 percent tax bracket. This way, Bob can convert $100,000 a year from his IRA to his Roth IRA and use some of the converted money to pay the extra tax bill. Since Helen is done converting, they stay in the 24 percent bracket.

STEP 6: HELEN RETIRES

At age sixty-three, Helen is downsized at work. She decides she's had enough anyway and would like to retire ahead of the original plan of being age sixty-five. She rolls over her traditional 401(k) from work to her now empty IRA and transfers her after-tax contribution account at work into her Roth (with contributions to her Roth and the growth from those contributions to her IRA).

Without her income from work, the couple has more room in the 24 percent tax bracket to apply the Roth conversion strategy to Helen's IRA again. They convert and pay the taxes on her IRA over the two years remaining, until they both fully retire at age sixty-five.

STEP 7: BOB RETIRES

Now the couple are both sixty-five, and full retirement is here. Let's take a look at what they have:

$2,000,000 in Helen's Roth IRA

+ $0 in Helen's IRA, as she managed to convert everything over the past fifteen years

+ $1,900,000 in Bob's Roth IRA, which is $100,000 less than Helen's because of the 72(t) payments

+ $500,000 in Bob's IRA, as he never got his old traditional 401(k) money converted

+ $50,000 in the non-qualified mutual fund account as an emergency fund

= $4,450,000 of total assets at age sixty-five, with only $500,000 in the tax-deferred bucket

STRUCTURING THE INCOME

Bob and Helen have done well restructuring their assets and shifting money from the tax-deferred bucket to the tax-free bucket as they approached retirement. Let's take a look at their income stream in retirement and compare the extra tax they paid over the past fifteen years to what they will save over the course of their retirement. Do you think what they did was worth it?

AGE SIXTY-FIVE TO SIXTY-NINE

During this portion of retirement, Bob and Helen will hold off on taking their Social Security so it will continue to grow until they reach age seventy, when they will be eligible to receive their maximum benefits.

Bob and Helen are able to take out at least $27,800 (the 2021 standard deduction plus the extra standard deduction for seniors) from Bob's IRA and receive this money tax-free by applying the standard deduction. The amount of the standard deduction is linked to inflation and rises over time, so realistically, by the time Bob and Helen reach age sixty-five, the standard deduction is likely to be closer to $37,000 a year. Whatever the amount, this is what they withdraw from Bob's IRA without tax.

They are now able to take as much from their Roth IRAs as they would like without the worry of taxes. They want to be extra conservative and follow a 3 percent rule for withdrawal of income from their Roth IRAs, along with a 3 percent raise each year to keep up with inflation. They are interested in leaving a legacy to their church and a charity one day, so they would like to have some money left at the end of their lives. This gives them $117,000 of income from the Roth accounts (a 3 percent withdrawal from a $3,900,000 balance).

Their income at age sixty-five is $144,800 ($27,800 from

IRAs and $117,000 from Roth accounts), all tax-free. This is actually *more* take-home income than while they were working, so they have an increase in their standard of living as they move into full retirement. Here is what Bob and Helen were taking home each year while working:

$240,000 Combined income from work

– $12,000 Bob's Roth 401(k) annual contribution

– $12,000 Helen's after-tax 401(k) contribution

– $11,720 FICA tax on their income

– $40,093 Federal tax (24 percent marginal bracket, 16.71 percent effective rate)

– $9,982 State tax (assuming Colorado as an example, with a 4.63 percent state tax)

– $24,000 Mortgage payment (paid off at retirement)

= $130,205 Annual take-home pay while working

AGE SEVENTY: SOCIAL SECURITY STARTS

Bob and Helen will each receive $2,500 a month, for a total of $30,000 a year from Social Security. Half of this eats up most of the threshold of their allowable provisional income before Social Security starts becoming taxable. For a married couple, 50 percent of their Social Security benefit becomes taxable once provisional income reaches $32,000. There isn't much room to withdraw from Bob's IRA and utilize the standard deduction to receive this money tax-free. Bob and Helen are also aware that RMDs are right around the corner, and they will be required to take money from the IRA. The RMD amount will put them over the threshold, and their Social Security would no longer be tax-free. Let's see what they do.

For now, even with Social Security, they are still income tax-free and receive about $193,000 in tax-free income. This is made up of:

> $131,000 from Roth withdrawals (a 3 percent withdrawal rate with a 3 percent raise each year)
> + $60,000 of Social Security income
> + $2,000 from Bob's IRA (offset by the standard deduction)
> = $193,000 of total income, tax-free.

This is over $5,000 more each month than they took home while still working! Well done!

GIFTING STRATEGIES

Bob and Helen are thrilled with almost $200,000 of tax-free income and are living their best lives. They have decided they do not want to give any money to the IRS, and nothing would please them more than to start gifting their tax-deferred money to their church and charities while they are still around. They want to see their money put to good use.

Once they are mandated to begin RMDs from Bob's IRA at

age seventy-two, they choose to gift those RMDs directly to charity, allowing them to exclude the income and not pay taxes on the money. They do this by having their advisor send the RMD payment directly to the charities, so the money doesn't pass through Bob and Helen. This also allows them to remain owners, keep control of what's left in the IRA, and gift the RMD amount each year. This is just in case they need this extra money for something important, such as long-term care.

HOW DID THEY DO?

The big question is: Was all that planning, shifting, and paying taxes really worth it?

Bob and Helen did pay a lot of taxes from age fifty to sixty-five by following this plan. However, they paid the tax on their terms, in a strategically controlled way and at known rates they were happy with. Let's look at how much they paid in taxes and lost in tax deductions before reaching retirement.

> $72,000 for the cost in Step 2, converting to a Roth account
> + $105,000 for costs in Step 4, the 72(t) withdrawals and conversions
> + $72,000 for the costs of more conversions in Step 5
> + $96,000 for costs in Step 6, (Helen retiring and converting her old 401(k) to a Roth account)

= $345,000 in taxes

+ $80,640 in lost tax deductions (Step 1 costs)

=$425,640 in total tax costs

Some people will point out that if they had stayed on their original path, they would have had more money in their accounts than they ended up with under this plan. This is because they wouldn't have paid that extra $345,000 in taxes or lost out on the tax deductions they were receiving. This is true, and a great point. Let's consider it.

If you added all the extra taxes Bob and Helen paid before retirement back into their plan plus the growth on this money, we can calculate they would have had about $500,000 more at age sixty-five. This means they would have had a balance of about $5 million (rounded up to be even more conservative) in their tax-deferred accounts instead of the $4,450,000 they ended up with. How would that have worked out?

This chart shows their income each year over twenty-five years of retirement, and what the tax would have been had all of it been taxable as per their original plan. This was created using the federal tax calculator which can be found in the Resources section of Divorce-The-IRS.com.

Year	Withdrawal	Taxes	Marginal Bracket	Effective Tax Rate
1	$150,000.00	$19,349.00	22.00%	12.90%
2	$154,500.00	$20,339.00	22.00%	13.16%
3	$159,135.00	$21,359.00	22.00%	13.42%
4	$163,909.05	$22,409.00	22.00%	13.67%
5	$168,826.32	$23,491.00	22.00%	13.91%
6	$173,891.11	$24,605.00	22.00%	14.15%
7	$179,107.84	$25,753.00	22.00%	14.38%
8	$184,481.08	$26,935.00	22.00%	14.60%
9	$190,015.51	$28,152.00	22.00%	14.82%
10	$195,715.98	$29,465.00	24.00%	15.05%
11	$201,587.46	$30,874.00	24.00%	15.32%
12	$207,635.08	$32,325.00	24.00%	15.57%
13	$213,864.13	$33,820.00	24.00%	15.81%
14	$220,280.06	$35,360.00	24.00%	16.05%
15	$226,888.46	$36,946.00	24.00%	16.28%
16	$233,695.11	$38,580.00	24.00%	16.51%
17	$240,705.97	$40,262.00	24.00%	16.73%
18	$247,927.14	$41,995.00	24.00%	16.94%
19	$255,364.96	$43,781.00	24.00%	17.14%
20	$263,025.91	$45,619.00	24.00%	17.34%
21	$270,916.69	$47,513.00	24.00%	17.54%
22	$279,044.19	$49,464.00	24.00%	17.73%
23	$287,415.51	$51,473.00	24.00%	17.91%
24	$296,037.98	$53,542.00	24.00%	18.09%
25	$304,919.12	$55,674.00	24.00%	18.26%
Totals	**$5,468,889.65**	**$879,085.00**		

The 3 percent withdrawal on $5 million would have been $150,000 in their first year of retirement. After applying the standard deduction, federal taxes owed would have been $19,349, and their actual spendable income would have only been $130,651. This is $14,149 less than what they had tax-free under the new plan. That's a difference of over $1,000 a month in retirement income! This gap would have only grown each year of their retirement, and once you added in Social Security and state tax, they would have paid a lot more in taxes. It's not even close.

As you can see, the $345,000 they paid in extra tax leading up to retirement, as well as the $80,640 they gave up in tax deductions, was more than worth the savings of almost $900,000 in just federal taxes during retirement. If you calculate the state taxes they would have owed (assuming they live in a state with state tax) and consider the fact that 85 percent of their Social Security income would have also been taxable at 24 percent under their old plan (they would have owed $14,400 in tax just on their Social Security the first year they received it), it's apparent the new plan was massively in their best interest!

This doesn't count the substantial tax savings they receive by gifting to two charities, and the tax-free legacy they will leave at the end of their lives.

What would have happened if tax rates had increased somewhere along the way during Bob and Helen's retirement? This would have dramatically increased their tax bills and compounded the negative effects had they continued on their original path. With the new plan, any tax rate increase would have no effect on their income.

The last point worth making in this case study is Tax Time Bomb 7, which can happen when the first spouse passes.

Had one partner passed sometime during retirement, the remaining spouse would have lost only one Social Security check worth of income and nothing else. The remaining accounts would have been combined into the surviving spouse's accounts without taxes, and income would have continued unaffected by the new, single tax brackets or lower standard deduction. Had this happened under the couple's original plan with everything in tax-deferred accounts, it would have been a *much* bigger tax problem for the remaining spouse to deal with.

In this case study, we saw that even though Bob and Helen started planning for retirement when they were closer to the finish line rather than the starting line, they were still able to use the principles in this book. With careful planning, they defused the tax time bombs that threatened to explode their savings and were able to keep significantly more money from the IRS to enjoy in retirement. However, neither Bob nor Helen had a problem that you might face. Neither of them had a pension.

Chapter 19

CASE STUDY 3

THE PENSION PROBLEM

Although pensions are becoming increasingly rare, especially in the corporate sector, there are still those who will receive a lifetime pension in retirement. These people usually worked for the federal or state government or the military.

> The problem with pensions is they are taxable income—they come from a tax-deferred bucket and are also considered provisional income.

This means if your pension income will be greater than your standard deduction, it will be impossible to avoid all tax in retirement. If your pension income will be less than your standard deduction, it may be possible to still pay no tax in retirement, although this will depend on the amount of your Social Security benefit.

Knowing you will have a pension in retirement should cause a shift in your planning. Since you will have guaranteed income every month from the pension that will go against your standard deduction as provisional income, your ideal number—the amount you should have in your tax-deferred bucket—will be reduced considerably. When your pension is equal to or larger than your standard deduction, your ideal number will always be $0 in your tax-deferred bucket. This makes the strategies in this book even more important to those who will receive a pension one day.

The government has helped with planning for this situation a bit by introducing the Roth TSP account. Available now to all military and most federal employees who may receive a pension one day, this account works just like the Roth 401(k). Unfortunately, you are not permitted to convert any money you may have in the traditional TSP program to the Roth TSP program while still employed, but you can switch your future contributions to the Roth TSP program at any time. It is also possible, once you are no longer employed by the agency offering you the TSP, to roll over your traditional TSP into an IRA. You can then convert that money into a Roth IRA and pay the taxes due (see the chapter on Roth strategies).

If you know you will receive a pension in retirement, the key is to work with a financial planner to understand if your income will be greater than your standard deduction and how that impacts your ideal number. Then, form a plan to shift your money into a Roth IRA or Roth TSP if necessary so you will pay the minimum taxes due in retirement.

I hope the case studies in these three chapters show that however close you are to the finish line of retirement, you have options to reduce the amount of taxes you will pay. You can even divorce the IRS completely, paying $0 tax over the span of your retirement.

In the final chapters, we will discuss specific considerations for Americans working (or thinking of retirement) overseas and for foreign nationals in America. Then, we'll get into final thoughts on defusing your tax time bombs and divorcing the IRS. If neither of these subjects apply (or are interesting) to you, please just skip over them to the conclusion, where we will wrap up all this information.

Chapter 20

AMERICANS OVERSEAS

If you are an American living or working overseas or thinking about retiring abroad, you may be wondering how the concepts in this book might differ for you. Misunderstandings abound when it comes to US taxes and living abroad. A lot of Americans erroneously believe that once you leave the United States, you also leave its tax jurisdiction. That's how it works with most of the world, but not with the United States. However, there can be some opportunities for Americans abroad, as well as some pitfalls.

ROTH CONVERSION OPPORTUNITY FOR AMERICANS OVERSEAS

Americans working or living overseas who plan to return to the United States in the future have Roth conversion strategy opportunities worth considering. Although still required to pay federal income tax in the United States on income earned even while living overseas, Americans do not generally have to pay any state income taxes while abroad. This creates an even more attractive scenario for using Roth conversion strategies.

AN EXAMPLE FROM THE SMITHS

Recently, the Smiths moved from California to Dubai for a five-year work contract. Mrs. Smith works full time as an engineer and earns a salary of $250,000, while Mr. Smith watches the kids and helps plan all the travel and adventures they want to take advantage of while living on a new continent. Their combined income puts them in the 24 percent federal income tax bracket in the US.

While overseas, the Smiths are not required to pay California state income tax. However, they are subject to federal income tax on income above the Foreign Earned Income Tax Exclusion (FEIE) limits. Upon completion of the contract overseas, they plan to move back to California. When they do, they will once again be subject to California state income taxes.

This creates an opportunity for the Smiths they would not have had if they were still living and working in California. Besides all the other benefits you have learned about in this book, the Smiths can execute Roth conversions while overseas and not pay any California state income tax on the money. The Smiths would be in the 9.3 percent marginal state tax bracket if they were living in California. This makes the Roth conversion a way to earn money in California that will never be taxed by the state. That can amount to significant savings.

For you, the size of this benefit will depend on which state you call home. For states with no income tax (there are seven) or low income tax, this isn't a big benefit. But for the moderate and high-income tax states (such as California, New York, and Oregon), this can lead to significant tax savings and benefits. Of course, all the other benefits listed in this book also apply.

RETIREMENT OVERSEAS

More and more Americans are looking at the option of retirement overseas. Lifestyle arbitrage, a term coined by Tim Ferris, the bestselling author of *The 4-Hour Workweek*, is the concept of stretching your hard-earned dollars in lower-cost environments that can be found in many countries around the world. While this is a great idea, and your dollars can definitely go further in some places, those who are globally minded need to carefully consider the concepts in this book.

Most countries around the world, both with and without US

tax treaties, tax their residents on income earned anywhere in the world. This is how it works in the United States as well. Where the problem lies is that many countries don't extend the same tax benefits to certain accounts we enjoy while inside the United States.

Most of this issue is well outside the scope of this book. I just want to warn those who like the ideas in this book and are thinking about an overseas retirement to be extra careful. Do more research and planning (or hire an expat-specific financial advisor like myself) before heading off and taking advantage of that lifestyle arbitrage.

What if you moved to Japan (or Australia, or Germany, or many other places) for retirement? The Roth IRA does not receive the same tax treatment there as it does in the United States. Although your distribution would be tax-free in the US, it would be taxed as a regular, taxable account in Japan (or any of the other countries mentioned), and you would owe taxes on any Roth IRA growth on your Japanese tax return. Most countries around the world treat a Roth IRA exactly this way.

Maybe you believe you won't get caught in Japan, or you can avoid paying the taxes there through some other means. Maybe you can get away with it, and maybe you can't. The penalties are stiff, though, if you are caught. It has become increasingly difficult to get away with global tax evasion since the passage of the Foreign Account Tax Compliance Act (FATCA) legislation in 2010. This law requires that all non-US banks and financial institutions report your accounts to the IRS if they know you are a US national or subject to tax in America. You are also required to report your foreign bank accounts to the IRS each year using the Foreign Bank Account Reporting (FBAR) form.

It is not my intent to scare you away from retirement abroad. Please just carefully consider the tax consequences before you make the leap. Diligent planning is necessary to retire abroad and maximize that lifestyle arbitrage.

INVESTING OVERSEAS

I have met more than one person who, when discussing the issues covered in this book, has told me they would like to move (or worse, has already moved) their money overseas. They hope that if the money is outside the US, they can avoid paying taxes on it. This is not the case and is a really bad idea.

Not all overseas investments are considered equal under IRS laws in America. And just reporting your overseas investments on the FBAR doesn't satisfy all the requirements if you hold something called a Passive Foreign Investment Company (PFIC). These are any type of pooled investment vehicle registered outside of the United States and include:

- Mutual funds not registered in the US (even if the fund company is from the US).
- ETFs not registered in the US.
- Foreign pensions or retirement schemes.
- Tax-sheltered investments in tax havens like the Isle of Man or Cyprus.
- Non-US cash value life insurance.
- Non-US money markets.

It's easy to find funds that appear to be identical in other countries and the US, such as the Vanguard 500 index. However, they are *not* the same fund. The Vanguard 500 indexes may be managed by the same company, but the US and the foreign versions are legally different funds. If you are a US expat, for example, and you own the European version of a Vanguard fund, you own a PFIC and have created a tax nightmare for yourself.

Any fund in Europe that is also considered an Undertakings for the Collective Investment in Transferable Securities (UCITS) fund will be considered a PFIC for US tax purposes as well. If you are a US expat, you are still subject to US taxation, and you should avoid UCITS and PFICs.

The requirements for reporting and paying taxes on these types of investments are extremely time-consuming and tax toxic. The IRS estimates that it takes about twenty-two hours of filing paperwork to report each PFIC that is owned by a US taxpayer. And the tax rates for PFICs can be over 50 percent. Certain laws were created to stop US citizens from hiding money overseas and trying to avoid paying taxes. The tax reporting requirements for PFICs are included in the Resources section of Divorce-The-IRS.com, if you would like to take a look.

Again, I don't want to scare anyone away from retiring or investing overseas. However, you must understand the opportunities and pitfalls before you move money outside of the US so you don't incur penalties or fines. There are many ways to avoid paying more taxes than necessary, but hiding money overseas is not a smart—or legal—strategy. If you want to move money to take advantage of lifestyle arbitrage and make your dollars go further, understand the impact on your tax situation, and create a plan to manage it.

Now let's examine the flip side: what is the tax situation for foreign nationals working in America?

Chapter 21

FOREIGN NATIONALS WORKING IN AMERICA

If you are a non-US citizen living and working in the United States, you face many new challenges in learning and understanding a new financial and tax system. Pension plans, taxation of income (both here and abroad), investments, retirement accounts, and estate planning considerations can seem overwhelming. Not understanding these often leads to inaction or mistakes.

Moving overseas can be exciting yet overwhelming. You probably moved to the United States for a job, an adventure, and new experiences. Some of the issues in this book are amplified if you are a foreign national working in the United States. This chapter is specifically written to help you avoid the costly pitfalls that many expats in the US experience.

Let's start with a brief overview of taxes for foreign nationals living as expats within the United States.

DETERMINING RESIDENCY

There are two categories in the United States that aliens (the IRS term for foreign nationals) fall into for tax purposes: resident or nonresident. If you are not a US citizen, you are automatically considered a nonresident alien unless you hold a Green Card or meet the substantial presence test.

Here is the definition of substantial presence from the IRS website:

> You will be considered a United States resident for tax purposes if you meet the substantial presence test for the calendar year. To meet this test, you must be physically present in the United States (U.S.) on at least:

1. 31 days during the current year, and
2. 183 days during the 3-year period that includes the current year and the 2 years immediately before that, counting:
   - All the days you were present in the current year, and
   - 1/3 of the days you were present in the first year before the current year, and
   - 1/6 of the days you were present in the second year before the current year.

There are more details of these definitions in the Resources section of Divorce-The-IRS.com.

Let's imagine you were physically present in the US for 120 days a year in 2017, 2018, and 2019. To determine if you meet the substantial presence test for 2019, count the full 120 days of presence in 2019, 40 days in 2018 (one-third of 120), and 20 days in 2017 (one-sixth of 120). Since the total for the three-year period is 180 days, you are not considered a resident under the substantial presence test for 2019.

Like most countries, you have to pay taxes in the United States if you are living and working within the United States. Like many countries, you also have to pay taxes on your worldwide income while living in the United States. What is different about the US, though, is that it has a citizen-based taxation system. This means if you are a US citizen or permanent resident, like a Green Card holder, you must pay taxes in America on worldwide income regardless of where you are living.

A COMMON MISTAKE

Many people don't realize they need to report and pay taxes on bank accounts and investments in their home country (or anywhere in the world) while living and working in the United States.

This is the first and one of the biggest mistakes that expats make in America. This is also something many people are not happy about while living and working in America. What do your bank account and investments back in your home country have to do with your work in America? Nothing, to be honest, but this is how the system works here, unfortunately. This is an important issue to consider before accepting a job in the United States, and it does stop some people from coming to live in America.

If you have bank and investment accounts totaling more than $10,000 in aggregate during any day of the year, anywhere in the world, you are required to report those bank and investment accounts to the IRS using the FBAR. You can read more about the FBAR in the Resources section of Divorce-The-IRS.com, but it's due to the IRS by April 15 of the following year.

Many people do not realize this requirement or choose not to report their accounts overseas. This is risky and can lead to very large penalties, and the chances of getting caught became much higher with the passage of the FATCA, which is also detailed, along with its penalties, in the Resources section of Divorce-The-IRS.com. This law requires that all non-US banks and financial institutions report your accounts to the IRS if they know you are a US national or subject to tax in the United States. Some people get away with not reporting their overseas assets, but as the world becomes more connected, this has become increasingly difficult.

According to the IRS, the penalty for not reporting your overseas income, bank accounts, or investment accounts is:

> A civil penalty of $10,000 for each nonwillful violation. But if your violation is found to be willful, the penalty is the greater of $100,000 or 50 percent of the amount in the account for each violation. Each year you didn't file is a separate violation.

TAX-TOXIC INVESTMENTS

Another common mistake is failing to get rid of tax-toxic investments like PFICs before coming to the United States.

Not all overseas investments are considered equal under the laws of the IRS in America. And just reporting your overseas investments on the FBAR doesn't satisfy all the requirements if you hold a PFIC. As we discussed in the previous chapter, these are any type of pooled investment vehicle registered outside of the United States and include:

- Mutual funds not registered in the US (even if the fund company is from the US).
- ETFs not registered in the US.
- Foreign pensions or retirement schemes.

- Tax-sheltered investments in tax havens like the Isle of Man or Cyprus.
- Non-US cash value life insurance.
- Non-US money markets.

More details on PFICs are included in the Resources section of Divorce-The-IRS.com.

As I warned Americans in the last chapter, it's easy to find funds that appear to be identical in both Europe and the US, such as the Vanguard 500 index. However, they are *not* the same fund. They may be managed by the same company, but legally, the US and European versions are different funds. If you are a European living in America, and you own the European version of a Vanguard fund, you own a PFIC and have created a tax nightmare for yourself.

Any fund in Europe that is also considered a UCITS (Undertakings for the Collective Investment in Transferable Securities) fund will be considered a PFIC for US tax purposes. If you are living in the US and subject to US taxation, you should avoid UCITS and PFICs.

As with Americans living overseas, the requirements for reporting and paying taxes on these types of investments are extremely time-consuming and tax toxic for foreign nationals. In case you skipped the last chapter, here is the key number: the IRS estimates that it takes about twenty-two hours of filing paperwork to report each PFIC that is owned by a US taxpayer. And the tax rates for PFICs can be over 50 percent. You can find the tax reporting requirements for PFICs in the Resources section of Divorce-The-IRS.com, if you would like to take a look.

These laws were not created to make your life difficult (although they can). They are an attempt to stop US citizens from hiding money overseas and avoiding taxes. Even so, they make life very difficult for expats living and working in the United States and should be handled very carefully.

YOUR EMPLOYER'S RETIREMENT PLAN (401(K), 403B, SEP, PENSION, AND SO ON)

Almost all companies in America that hire expats offer some type of retirement savings plan that you may be able to participate in while working in the United States. As you learned earlier in this book, the most common form of retirement plan is called the 401(k). How you handle your participation in a 401(k) plan (or any employer-sponsored retirement plan) while you are working in America can have a big impact on how much of that money you get to take home with you one day.

The 401(k) plan, in its simplest form, is just a savings account you may elect to contribute some of your salary to each pay period. The plan offers several different investments to choose from, usually mutual funds, which you can learn about in the Resources section of Divorce-The-IRS. com. The different investments range from very conservative to very aggressive based on the stock market.

A key point to remember is that you are always fully vested in the contributions *you* put into a 401(k) (or other retirement plan) in America. This means you own the money, 100 percent.

On top of any money you choose to put into the retirement plan at work, your employer will also usually contribute to the plan to help you save more toward retirement. This is typically called a match. This can be a set dollar amount but is usually a percentage of your salary. You may have to work for a company for a certain period of time before you become vested in this portion of the money and it actually becomes yours. If you are not vested in some or all of the money your employer has contributed on your behalf when your employment ends, your employer gets to keep that portion of the account.

TRADITIONAL 401(K) OR ROTH 401(K)?

Most of this book has advocated for the Roth 401(k) to help you avoid borrowing from the IRS and grow your money tax-free. This is generally best for Americans, but what if you don't plan on staying in America and would like to take your money with you when you leave? Which choice is best for expats working in America?

People commonly misunderstand the difference between traditional and Roth options in their employer's retirement plan and select the wrong choice based on future goals. Below, we'll examine how each one works.

TRADITIONAL PLAN

This plan has been around the longest and is the most utilized in America. This doesn't mean it is automatically the best choice for you, though! A traditional plan allows you to put your money in *before* you pay taxes on it. Many people like this option because it offers them tax savings today. They pay fewer taxes today by putting money into the plan before paying taxes on that money.

Not only does your money go into this plan before you pay any taxes, once it is in the plan, it grows tax-deferred as well. This means you don't pay taxes on any of the interest or growth from your investments until retirement, or when you take the money out. The United States government has set the retirement age for these plans at 59.5 years old. This doesn't mean you have to retire at that age; it just means you have to keep your money in the plan until 59.5 to receive all the benefits of tax deferral.

If you do take money out of a traditional plan before you turn 59.5 years old, you will have to pay taxes as if you earned the money at your job, plus a 10 percent penalty for early withdrawal. These rules generally make the traditional plan the incorrect choice for expats in America who do not plan on becoming citizens and remaining in the United States permanently. We've seen many expats want to take their retirement money with them when they depart America, only to lose almost 50 percent of their account balance to taxes and penalties. Ouch!

ROTH PLAN

The Roth is a newer plan in America that allows you to invest some of your salary from work in the same 401(k) account, but *after* your money has been taxed. This means you pay tax on your earnings and then save it in the Roth 401(k). This does not give you the benefit of immediate tax savings—something most Americans are after—but it does have several benefits for expats you should understand.

Because you put your money into the Roth plan after taxes, the money grows tax-free. If you wait until that magical age of 59.5, you are able to withdraw your money—all your money, including any interest or growth from the investments—completely tax-free! This is a considerable benefit to both Americans and expats who can delay gratification.

It's a trade-off: small tax savings today for no tax obligations later in life. This is usually the best option for expats.

If you do decide to take your money when you leave America and you are not 59.5 years old, you will only pay taxes or penalties on any interest or growth the account has earned. You will never pay any further taxes or penalties on the money you contributed while you were working. This can make a huge difference in the amount of money you are able to take with you when you finish your American adventure! Let's look at an example of two expats.

Chris and Martina both came to America to work at the same company three years ago. They started on the same day and went through the same orientation. Chris chooses to put 10 percent of his salary into the traditional 401(k) plan the company offers. Martina chooses to put the same 10 percent of her salary into the Roth plan. The expats make the exact same salary of $100,000 a year and put in the same amount of money. In this graphic, we can see how it works out for them.

A Tale of Two Expats

Our story begins with two expats, each contributing 10%
of their $100K per year salary to a retirement plan for 3 years.
The company also contributes 5% each year as a match.

CHRIS

Chooses to invest savings
into the traditional 401(k)
plan the company offers.

Contributions from salary	$30,000
5% of his salary matched by the company over 3 years	$15,000
Earns 5% interest on the investments	$4,651
Amount in traditional plan at end of year 3	**$49,652**
Tax savings over 3 years	$6,600

MARY

Chooses to invest savings
into the Roth plan.

Contributions from salary	$30,000
5% of her salary matched by the company over 3 years	$15,000
Earns 5% interest on the investments	$4,651
Amount in Roth plan at end of year 3	**$49,652**
Tax savings over 3 years	$0

Time to Leave America and Take the Money

What happens when they withdraw their entire
balance before they reach 59.5 years old?

Initial Withdrawal	$49,652
Tax owed on the balance (income puts expat into the 24% tax bracket)	$11,916
10% penalty owed for being under 59.5 years old	$4,965
Amount IRS takes when he leaves	$16,881
+$6,600 received in tax savings over the 3 years working in America (which he didn't save as it was just a bit more in each paycheck every month)	
How much money actually goes home	**$32,771**

Initial Withdrawal	$49,652
Tax owed on the balance (only owed on the $4,651 of interest)	$1,023
10% penalty owed (only owed on the $4,651 of interest)	$465
Amount IRS takes when she leaves	$1,488
No tax savings on paycheck each month	
How much money actually goes home	**$48,164**

 KEY POINT

The Roth plan with your employer is almost always the better choice for expats working in America!

We can see that Martina, who invested her money into a Roth account, takes home significantly more money than Chris, who used a traditional 401(k). An employer's Roth plan is almost always the better choice for expats working in America.

SOCIAL SECURITY

Probably similar to the country you moved from, there is a government-run, old-age pension scheme in America. It is called Social Security. This provides a monthly pension to retirees in America, starting between the ages of sixty-two (with a reduced amount) and seventy (the maximum amount).

You and everyone working for a company in America will contribute 6.2 percent of your salary to this pension scheme. This is a mandatory tax in America, and you cannot opt out of it. You will also pay an additional 1.45 percent of your salary in Medicare tax for the old-age government health insurance. This payment is also mandatory.

Unfortunately, you cannot apply to get any of this tax money back if you decide to leave the United States. Unless you plan to stay and work for more than ten years (the minimum amount of time you have to pay into this system to be eligible for a benefit), you won't receive any benefit from paying these taxes in America.

If you do end up staying in America long term, this benefit can become very valuable to you. The United States also has treaty agreements with many other countries, called totalization agreements, which allow you to receive or transfer your benefit in America to your home country's retirement pension scheme. See the Resources section of

Divorce-The-IRS.com for more information on totalization agreements.

INVESTING WHILE IN THE UNITED STATES

Many people do not understand or take advantage of the tax treaty benefits that may be applicable when investing in the United States.

As I write, the United States has income tax treaties with sixty-seven foreign countries, which you can read about in the Resources section of Divorce-The-IRS.com. Under these treaties, residents of foreign countries both in America and abroad may be eligible to be taxed at a reduced rate or exempt from US income taxes on certain items of income they receive from sources within the United States. These reduced rates and exemptions vary among countries and specific items of income.

If your home country has a tax treaty or totalization agreement with the United States, this could be an advantage to you. Many treaties between the US and European Union (EU) countries allow tax-advantaged investing for EU citizens in the United States. Germans, for example, pay no tax on capital gains from stock investments. Income from many debt instruments like bonds is also tax-free for Europeans in the United States.

It is common to misunderstand the increased safety and regulation, and lower fees and liquidity provided by investing in the United States. There is no financial market in the world that has the regulation, scale, liquidity, or low fee structure like America does. This makes utilizing American financial markets for investing very attractive to both foreigners living in and outside of America. Although fees have been decreasing significantly all over the world, America is still the least expensive place to invest, the most highly regulated (making it the most protected from scams), and has the most liquidity. There is a link to the Morningstar research on worldwide fees in the Resources section of Divorce-The-IRS.com.

Utilizing American financial markets does not mean you will invest only in America or in American companies, although you can do that. Almost every major, publicly traded corporation worldwide is available for purchase in the American financial markets. Companies realize America has the biggest financial market in the world, and they issue shares and bonds in this country.

> You can use American financial markets to build a completely European stock and bond portfolio with lower fees, more liquidity, and greater safety than you could in Europe.

For this reason, many expats working in America choose to

bring the money they've invested in their home country to the United States. Once they understand how the financial markets work in America, as well as the tax treaty benefits, they realize they can be more tax- and cost-efficient while building their wealth faster within the American financial system.

Many expats also choose to leave their investments in America, even after they have departed. This is due in part to the ease of managing investments online these days and because it is more tax- and cost-efficient to do so. Finding and building a relationship with a trusted, expat-specific financial advisor can help, as many expats feel better about leaving their money in the American financial system if they are working with a trusted advisor who can oversee everything.

As a foreign national working in America, your tax considerations can seem overwhelming, but there are many opportunities to take advantage of and ways to avoid the pitfalls of investing money here and overseas. Make sure you are informed so you can enjoy these benefits.

CONCLUSION

If you have never been in love with paying taxes and like the idea of strategically setting yourself up to divorce the IRS when you retire, then I hope you liked this book. It has outlined, simply, how to start planning your exit from taxes by highlighting the biggest tax time bombs that can go off in your life. The key to divorcing the IRS is getting the right amount of money into each of the three tax buckets through contribution or shifting strategies.

What is the perfect combination of accounts in the different tax buckets? It's different for everyone, but in general, keep the following in mind:

1. The "tax me now" bucket should hold about six months of income as an emergency fund to protect you from life's curveballs. This is also the place for any short-term

savings you need for big purchases, such as a down payment on a home or car.

2. The "tax me later" bucket should house any money you need to put into your traditional 401(k) to receive the full match from your employer. This is generally about the right amount of contribution—and nothing more—for this bucket. The goal is to have a balance at age seventy-two that will make your RMD equal to your standard deduction. Find your ideal number by using the calculator at Divorce-The-IRS.com.

3. Everything else should be shifted or added and accumulated in the "tax me never" bucket utilizing Roth accounts and, under the right circumstances, cash value life insurance (LIRPs).

At the end of the day, the cost of admission to a tax-free retirement and the 0 percent tax bracket is a willingness to pay the tax sooner rather than later. Many don't want to do this, but you will have to pay the tax no matter what (or your beneficiaries will). There is just no way around this!

Do you want to take control of your financial future and pay the IRS on *your* terms while we have known, historically low tax rates? Or do you want to be forced to pay taxes when the IRS mandates it in retirement at unknown, future tax rates? The choice, of course, is yours.

You are now aware of the eight biggest tax time bombs that

can explode. They are exploding tax rates, early withdrawal penalties, sharing your retirement with the IRS, Social Security tax, Medicare premiums, required minimum distributions, outliving your spouse, and paying taxes from the grave. However, all of these can be managed with smart strategies. You have seen examples of these strategies in action from people at various points along the journey to retirement. And you know the opportunities and pitfalls facing both Americans living overseas and foreign nationals working in the US.

Crafting a comprehensive financial plan that uses these strategies will defuse your tax time bombs. It will put you on track to be as close as possible to a 0 percent tax bracket in retirement and will take time and effort. If you think paying as little as possible to the IRS and maximizing your retirement income is worth it, you should take the time and make the effort to craft such a plan. As you can see from the examples in this book, the difference in the amount of lifetime tax paid is considerable.

Working with a good fiduciary financial and tax planner can certainly make this process easier and less worrisome. In my financial practices, Baobab Wealth (for those in the US) and Baobab Wealth Abroad (for those outside of the US), I help globally minded Americans and cross-border families around the world create real wealth for themselves and their families in tax efficient ways so they can maximize their dreams in life and beyond. I help these families use the strategies discussed in this book to form a plan, leaving them confident in their retirement strategy.

Whether you plan on your own or with the assistance of a fiduciary financial and tax planner, I hope you *do* craft a plan for retirement. Although it may feel tempting to ignore these tax time bombs, my clients consistently tell me they have incredible peace of mind from proactively defusing them—not to mention they save significant money.

I hope your plan helps you enjoy a relaxing, fulfilling, and tax-free retirement. And I wish you a wonderful divorce from the IRS!

ACKNOWLEDGMENTS

Writing a book is a difficult journey with many ups and downs along the way. I would have never completed this journey without the love and support of my wife, Sonja. From editing help to creative input and design, her influence and patience with this process were invaluable, and I am forever thankful.

Even if you know what to say and how to say it, words often need illustration to make their points and come to life. Without the help and input of my friend and marketing director, Dustin, none of the nonword content in this book would have been possible. Without Dustin's marketing expertise, you also may not have found this book. And for that, I am also grateful.

One of the reasons I am so passionate about helping people

with financial planning is because of my mom. She taught me the importance of saving and investing in the future from an early age. She has never stopped encouraging me, and without her support, this book never would have been written.

Without the discipline instilled in me by my dad to "make a plan and stick to it" (a very tough job), I never would have had what it took to start and complete this book. I am thankful every day for the excellent job my dad did in teaching me to work hard. I am trying to instill the same principles he taught me into his grandson, Hendrik.

It is always with an attitude of gratitude that I serve clients in my financial practice. These individuals and families have placed their trust and financial future in my hands, a responsibility I don't take lightly. I am thankful for every client relationship I have, as most of my clients become true friends as we journey together through life.

Although we have never met, I would like to thank Nick Murray. As the author of many great books written for financial professionals, Nick has been like a mentor to me throughout my career through his books, writings, and speaking events. The book *The Excellent Investment Advisor* is what I have based my entire career on, and I read it every time I need any guidance in this profession.

Another person whom I have never had the pleasure of meeting in person but has been very influential in my financial practice is Michael Kitces. A true thought leader in financial planning. I turn to Michael's research and resources often to serve my clients better. Please keep up the great work you are doing for our profession!

I would also like to thank the incredible team at Scribe who helped me get my first book ready to share with the world. The talent, thoughtfulness, patience, and professionalism shown to me from this team has been remarkable and has helped me make this book much better than I could have ever done on my own.

I also want to thank everyone else who played a role in shaping this book or my career, or has helped me out along the way. Without all of you, I wouldn't be who or where I am today.

ABOUT THE AUTHOR

Taxes are not the most exciting subject, and I never thought I would find myself writing about them, to be honest. They are a part of life, though, and more important than most people realize. We spend so much of our lives working just so we can pay an enormous amount of money to the government in the form of taxes.

As my financial practice and I matured over the years, I found myself working on tax planning more and more often as part of comprehensive planning for my clients. I realized this was one area that could make the biggest difference to my clients or the IRS in obtaining and retaining real wealth, but not both. Each year, I became more frustrated as I met people who would generally seek my counsel only after experiencing one or multiple tax explosions in their lives. It was often too late for them. I realized my purpose on earth is to try and help people live their best lives through proper financial planning. Keeping your money from the IRS is such a big part of that process.

Introduced to the expat lifestyle early on, I was born in Zambia to an adventurous American couple who traveled the world, as I grew up with a brother and a sister. My parents' wanderlust rubbed off on me, and I have spent most of my life as an expat now, traveling the world helping other Americans, both in the US and expats, obtain financial independence. I wrote this book in my home office in Moscow, Russia, only four hundred meters from Red Square and the Kremlin. This is just one of my homes and offices worldwide.

My mom's need to save for the future also rubbed off on me, and I am grateful every day for the time she took to educate me on financial matters from an early age. I didn't always listen, and I made my fair share of financial mistakes when I was younger, just like everyone does. But she never stopped telling me—and does to this day—how important it is to keep saving money and investing for the future.

My experiences have allowed me to learn not just about the American tax system (which taxes me on my worldwide income regardless of my location since I'm an American citizen) but other tax and financial systems around the world as well. This has given me a unique perspective on wealth and how taxes play into wealth creation and retention globally.

Happily married to a German citizen, Sonja, we have one son, Hendrik, who holds two passports and speaks two languages. We are a typical cross-border family with tax issues spanning multiple borders. We enjoy international travel, sailing, mountaineering, and spending time with those we consider to be true friends.

As the founder of Baobab Wealth and Baobab Wealth Abroad, I help both Americans and cross-border families around the world create real wealth for themselves and their families in tax efficient ways so they can maximize their dreams in life and beyond.

CPSIA information can be obtained
at www.ICGtesting.com
Printed in the USA
JSHW031949030421
13175JS00002B/6